COLLINS & BROWN

Iz

Thought this would be
GREAT for times in
your Brixton flat :)
Love Mark
xx

The expression Good Housekeeping as used in the
title of the book is the trademark of The National
Magazine Company and The Hearst Corporation,
registered in the United Kingdom and USA, and
other principal countries of the world, and is the
absolute property of The National Magazine
Company and The Hearst Corporation. The use
of this trademark other than with the express
permission of The National Magazine Company
or The Hearst Corporation is strictly prohibited.

The Good Housekeeping website is
www.goodhousekeeping.co.uk

ISBN 978-1-909397-01-9

A catalogue record for this book is available from
the British Library.

Reproduction by Dot Gradations Ltd, UK
Printed and bound by
1010 Printing International Ltd, China

This book can be ordered direct from the publisher.
Contact the marketing department, but try your
bookshop first.

www.anovabooks.com

Christmas 2013

NOTES

Both metric and imperial measures are given for
the recipes. Follow either set of measures, not a
mixture of both, as they are not interchangeable.

All spoon measures are level.
1 tsp = 5ml spoon; 1 tbsp = 15ml spoon.

Ovens and grills must be preheated to the specified
temperature.

Medium eggs should be used except where
otherwise specified. Free-range eggs are
recommended.

Note that some recipes contain raw or lightly
cooked eggs. The young, elderly, pregnant women
and anyone with an immune-deficiency disease
should avoid these because of the slight risk
of salmonella.

Contents

Dips and Breads

Mixed Italian Bruschetta

Hands-on time: 25 minutes

1 long thin French stick

400g can butter beans, drained and rinsed

a small handful of fresh mint, shredded

grated zest and juice of ½ lemon

2 tbsp extra virgin olive oil, plus extra to drizzle

seeds from ½ pomegranate

150g (5oz) cherry tomatoes, quartered

200g (7oz) mozzarella bocconcini, halved

1 tbsp fresh basil pesto

2 tbsp freshly chopped basil, plus extra leaves to garnish

a small handful of rocket

6 slices bresaola

15g (½oz) freshly shaved Parmesan

75g (3oz) roasted red pepper, sliced

2 tbsp black olive tapenade

salt and freshly ground black pepper

1 Cut the bread diagonally into 24 slices and toast in batches. Mash together the butter beans, mint, lemon zest and juice and oil. Season to taste with salt and ground black pepper and stir through most of the pomegranate seeds. Put to one side.

2 In a separate bowl, stir together the cherry tomatoes, mozzarella bocconcini, pesto and basil.

3 To assemble, spoon the bean mixture on to six toasts and garnish with the remaining pomegranate seeds. Top a further six with the mozzarella mixture and six with rocket, bresaola and Parmesan. Drizzle with the oil.

4 For the final six bruschetta, put a few slices of roasted pepper on each toast. Add a little tapenade and garnish with a basil leaf.

Serves 6

Red Pepper Pesto Croûtes

TAKE 5

🍴 **Hands-on time:** 20 minutes
Cooking time: about 20 minutes

1 thin French stick, sliced into 24 rounds

olive oil to brush

fresh pesto

4 pepper pieces (from a jar of marinated peppers), each sliced into 6 strips

pinenuts to garnish

1 Preheat the oven to 200°C (180°C fan oven) mark 6. Brush both sides of the bread slices with oil and put on a baking sheet. Cook in the oven for 15–20 minutes.

2 Spread 1 tsp pesto on each croûte, top with a pepper strip, then garnish with pinenuts and serve.

Serves 24

Lemon and Rosemary Olives

To serve six, you will need:
a few fresh rosemary sprigs, plus extra to garnish, 1 garlic clove, 175g (6oz) mixed black and green Greek olives, pared zest of 1 lemon, 2 tbsp vodka (optional), 300ml (½ pint) extra virgin olive oil.

1 Put the rosemary and garlic in a small heatproof bowl and pour over enough boiling water to cover. Leave for 1-2 minutes, then drain well.
2 Put the olives, lemon zest and vodka, if using, in a glass jar and add the rosemary and garlic. Pour over enough oil to cover the olives. Cover and chill for at least 24 hours before using.
3 To serve, remove the olives from the oil and garnish with sprigs of fresh rosemary. Use within one week.

SAVE MONEY

Don't waste the flavoured oil that's left over from the olives. It's perfect for using in salad dressings and marinades.

Tapenade

To serve four, you will need:
3 tbsp capers, rinsed and drained,
75g (3oz) pitted black olives, 50g
can anchovy fillets in oil, drained,
100ml (3½fl oz) olive oil, 2 tbsp
brandy, freshly ground black
pepper, vegetable sticks, grilled
vegetables or toasted French bread
to serve.

1 Put the capers into a blender or
   food processor with the olives
   and anchovies. Process briefly to
   chop.
2 With the motor running, add the
   oil in a steady stream. Stir in the
   brandy and season with pepper
   to taste. Transfer to a serving
   bowl.
3 Serve the tapenade with
   raw vegetable sticks, grilled
   vegetables or toasted French
   bread.

Houmous

To serve six, you will need:
400g can chickpeas, drained and rinsed, juice of 1 lemon, 4 tbsp tahini, 1 garlic clove, crushed, 5 tbsp extra virgin olive oil, salt and freshly ground black pepper, warm pitta bread (see page 20) or toasted flatbreads to serve.

1 Put the chickpeas, lemon juice, tahini, garlic and oil in a blender or food processor. Season generously with salt and ground black pepper, then whiz to a paste.
2 Spoon the hummus into a bowl, then cover and chill until needed.
3 Serve with warm pitta bread or toasted flatbreads.

Black Olive Houmous

Stir 25g (1oz) roughly chopped pitted black olives and 1 tsp paprika into the houmous paste. Sprinkle with a little extra paprika and extra virgin olive oil, if you like.

Black Olive Bread

To make two loaves, you will need:
2 tsp traditional dried yeast, 500g
(1lb 2oz) strong white bread flour,
plus extra to dust, 2 tsp coarse salt,
plus extra to sprinkle, 6 tbsp extra
virgin olive oil, plus extra to grease,
100g (3½oz) black olives, pitted
and chopped.

1   Put 150ml (¼ pint) hand-hot
    water into a jug, stir in the yeast
    and leave for 10 minutes or until
    frothy. Put the flour into a bowl
    or a food processor, then add
    the salt, yeast mix, 200ml (7fl
    oz) warm water and 2 tbsp oil.
    Using a wooden spoon or the
    dough hook, mix for 2–3 minutes
    to make a soft, smooth dough.
    Put the dough into a lightly oiled
    bowl, cover with oiled clingfilm
    and leave it in a warm place for
    45 minutes or until doubled in
    size.
2   Punch the dough to knock out
    the air, then knead on a lightly
    floured worksurface for 1 minute.
    Add the olives and knead until
    combined. Divide in half, shape
    into rectangles and put into two
    greased tins, each about 25.5
    × 15cm (10 × 6in). Cover with
    clingfilm and leave in a warm
    place for 1 hour or until the
    dough is puffy.
3   Preheat the oven to 200°C (180°C
    fan oven) mark 6. Press your
    finger into the dough 12 times,
    drizzle 2 tbsp oil over the surface
    and sprinkle with salt. Bake for
    30–35 minutes until golden.
    Drizzle with the remaining oil.
    Slice and serve while warm.

Classic Houmous

400g can chickpeas
40ml (1½fl oz) olive oil, plus extra
   to drizzle
1½ tsp lemon juice
1 small garlic clove
¼ tsp ground cumin
sprinkle of paprika or cayenne pepper
   (optional)
salt and freshly ground black pepper
breadsticks and toasted pitta bread
   (see page 20) to serve

1 Drain and rinse the chickpeas; put a spoonful to one side and put the rest into a food processor with the oil, lemon juice, 1 tbsp water, garlic clove, ground cumin and seasoning.

2 Whiz until smooth, then check the seasoning. Scrape into a serving dish. Garnish with the reserved chickpeas, a sprinkle of paprika or cayenne pepper (if you have it) and a drizzle of olive oil. Serve with breadsticks and toasted pitta bread for scooping.

Serves 6

Nan

🍴 **Hands-on time:** 20 minutes, plus rising
Cooking time: about 12 minutes

15g (½oz) fresh yeast or 1½ tsp
  traditional dried yeast
about 150ml (¼ pint) tepid milk
450g (1lb) plain white flour, plus extra
  to dust
1 tsp baking powder
½ tsp salt
2 tsp caster sugar
1 medium egg, beaten
2 tbsp vegetable oil, plus extra
  to grease
4 tbsp natural yogurt

1 Blend the fresh yeast with the milk.
  If using dried yeast, sprinkle it into
  the milk and leave in a warm place
  for 15 minutes or until frothy.

2 Sift the flour, baking powder and
  salt into a large bowl. Make a well
  in the centre and stir in the sugar,
  egg, oil and yogurt. Add the yeast
  liquid and mix well to a soft dough,
  adding more milk if necessary. Turn
  the dough out on to a lightly floured
  worksurface and knead well for 10
  minutes or until smooth and elastic.

3 Place the dough in a bowl, cover
  with oiled clingfilm and leave to
  rise in a warm place for about 1 hour
  until doubled in size.

4 Preheat the grill. Knead the dough
  on a lightly floured worksurface
  for 2–3 minutes, then divide into
  six equal-size pieces. Roll out
  each piece on a lightly floured
  worksurface and shape into a large
  teardrop about 25.5cm (10in) long.

5 Place a nan on a baking sheet and
  put under the hot grill. Cook for
  1½–2 minutes on each side until
  golden brown and puffy. Cook the
  remaining nan in the same way.
  Serve warm.

Makes 6

Pitta Bread

Hands-on time 20 minutes, plus rising
Cooking time: about 8 minutes per batch, plus cooling

15g (½oz) fresh yeast or
   1½ tsp traditional dried yeast and
   1 tsp sugar
700g (1½lb) strong white flour, plus
   extra to dust
1 tsp salt
1 tbsp caster sugar
1 tbsp olive oil, plus extra to grease

1 Blend the fresh yeast with 450ml (¾ pint) tepid water. If using dried yeast, sprinkle it into the water with the sugar and leave in a warm place for 15 minutes or until frothy.

2 Put the flour, salt and sugar into a bowl, make a well in the centre and pour in the yeast liquid with the oil. Mix to a smooth dough, then turn out on to a lightly floured worksurface and knead for 10 minutes or until smooth and elastic.

3 Place the dough in a large bowl, cover with oiled clingfilm and leave to rise in a warm place until doubled in size.

4 Divide the dough into 16 pieces and roll each into an oval shape about 20.5cm (8in) long. Place on floured baking sheets, cover with oiled clingfilm and leave in a warm place for about 30 minutes until slightly risen and puffy. Preheat the oven to 240°C (220°C fan oven) mark 9.

5 Bake the pittas in batches for 5–8 minutes only. They should be just lightly browned on top. Remove from the oven and wrap in a clean tea towel. Repeat with the remaining pittas.

6 When the pittas are warm enough to handle, but not completely cold, transfer them to a plastic bag and leave until cold. This will ensure that they have a soft crust.

7 To serve, warm in the oven, or toast lightly. Split and fill with salad, cheese, cold meats or your favourite sandwich filling. Or, cut into strips and serve with dips.

Makes 16

Tzatziki

To serve eight, you will need:
1 cucumber, 300g (11oz) Greek-style yogurt, 2 tsp olive oil, 2 tbsp freshly chopped mint, 1 large garlic clove, crushed, salt and freshly ground black pepper, warm pitta bread (see page 20) and vegetable sticks to serve.

1 Halve, seed and dice the cucumber and put into a bowl.
2 Add the yogurt and olive oil. Stir in the chopped mint and garlic, and season with salt and ground black pepper to taste. Cover and chill in the fridge until ready to serve.
3 Serve with warm pitta bread and vegetable sticks.

Taramasalata

To serve six, you will need:
100g (3½oz) country-style bread, crusts removed, 75g (3oz) smoked cod roe, 2 tbsp lemon juice, 100ml (3½fl oz) light olive oil, freshly ground black pepper, warm pitta bread (see page 20) or toasted flatbreads to serve.

1 Put the bread into a bowl, cover with cold water and leave to soak for 10 minutes. Drain and squeeze out most of the water.
2 Soak the smoked cod roe in cold water to cover for 10 minutes, then drain and remove the skin.
3 Put the roe in a blender or food processor with the bread and whiz for 30 seconds. With the motor running, add the lemon juice and oil, and whiz briefly to combine. Season with ground black pepper to taste.
4 Spoon into a bowl, cover and chill until needed. Serve with warm pitta bread or toasted flatbreads.

Blue Cheese Dip

To serve six, you will need:
150ml (¼ pint) soured cream, 1
garlic clove, crushed, 175g (6oz)
blue Stilton, juice of 1 lemon,
salt and freshly ground black
pepper, snipped chives to garnish,
vegetable sticks to serve.

1 Put all the ingredients into a
   blender or food processor and
   work to a smooth paste.
2 Transfer to a serving dish and
   chill until required. Check the
   seasoning, sprinkle with chives
   and serve with a selection of
   vegetable sticks.

Guacamole

To serve six, you will need:
2 ripe avocados, 2 small tomatoes,
seeded and chopped, juice of 2
limes, 2 tbsp extra virgin olive oil, 2
tbsp freshly chopped coriander, salt
and freshly ground black pepper,
tortilla chips or warm pitta bread
(see page 20) and vegetable sticks
to serve.

1 Cut the avocados in half, remove
   the stones and peel away the
   skin. Tip the flesh into a bowl
   and mash with a fork.
2 Quickly add the tomatoes, lime
   juice, oil and chopped coriander.
   Mix well and season with salt
   and ground black pepper to
   taste. Cover and chill until ready
   to serve.
3 Serve the guacamole with
   tortilla chips or warm pitta bread
   and vegetable sticks.

Red Pepper and Feta Dip

To make about 375g (13oz) (25 tbsp),
you will need:
290g jar roasted red peppers,
drained, 200g (7oz) feta, crumbled,
1 small garlic clove, 1 tbsp natural
yogurt and toasted pitta bread (see
page 20) to serve.

1 Put all the ingredients into a
   blender or food processor and
   whiz until smooth. Serve the dip
   with strips of toasted pitta bread.

Tortilla Chips for Dips

TAKE
5

Hands-on time: 10 minutes
Cooking time: about 20 minutes, plus cooling

8 flour tortillas
2 tbsp olive oil
¼–½ tsp smoked paprika
salt
dips to serve

SAVE TIME

Make up to two days ahead.
Keep in an airtight tin.

1 Preheat the oven to 200°C (180°C fan oven) mark 6. Stack the flour tortillas on top of each other, then cut through the stack like a pizza to make eight wedges. Put the triangles into a large bowl with the oil, smoked paprika and lots of salt.

2 Use your hands to mix everything together, making sure all the triangles are covered with oil and spice. Divide the triangles between two baking sheets.

3 Cook for 12–20 minutes, tossing occasionally, until golden and crisp. Leave to cool completely before serving with your favourite dips.

Serves 10

Quick Tomato

Put 4 roughly chopped tomatoes, ½ ripe, peeled and roughly chopped avocado, 1 tsp olive oil and the juice of ½ lime in a bowl and stir well. Use for grilled fish or chicken.

Smoky

Put 75g (3oz) finely chopped onions or shallots, 150ml (¼ pint) shop-bought barbecue sauce, 100ml (3½fl oz) maple syrup, 1 tbsp cider vinegar, 1 tbsp soft brown sugar, 100ml (3½fl oz) water, 1 tsp lemon juice and a little grated lemon zest in a pan. Bring to the boil and leave to bubble for 10–15 minutes until syrupy. Take the pan off the heat and add 6 finely chopped spring onions and 175g (6oz) finely chopped fresh pineapple. Serve warm or cold. Use for burgers.

Mango and Fennel

Put 1 halved and diced mango, 1 small trimmed and diced fennel bulb, 1 seeded and finely diced chilli (See Safety Tip, page 38), 1 tbsp balsamic vinegar, 2 tbsp freshly chopped flat-leafed parsley and 2 tbsp freshly chopped mint into a bowl. Add the juice of 1 lime, stir to combine and season generously with salt and ground black pepper. Use for grilled chicken.

Avocado, Tomato and Coriander

Put 1 chopped red onion in a bowl and add 1 ripe, peeled and chopped avocado, 4 large roughly chopped tomatoes, a small handful of roughly chopped fresh coriander and the juice of 1 lime. Mix well, then season with salt and ground black pepper. Use at once for grilled pork chops or chicken.

Prawn and Avocado

Put 2 large ripe, peeled and roughly chopped avocados in a large bowl, then add 350g (12oz) cooked, peeled king prawns, 6 small finely sliced spring onions, 3 tbsp freshly chopped coriander, the grated zest and juice of 3 limes and 8 tbsp olive oil. Mix well, then season with salt and ground black pepper. Use for smoked salmon or grilled fish.

Parmesan and Olive Grissini

Hands-on time: 20 minutes, plus kneading and rising
Cooking time: about 20 minutes, plus cooling

Bread Machine Recipe

1 tsp easy-blend dried yeast

500g (1lb 2oz) strong white bread flour, plus extra to dust

1 tsp salt

3 tbsp olive oil

2 tsp golden caster sugar

50g (2oz) pitted black olives, finely chopped

50g (2oz) Parmesan, freshly grated

To finish

oil to grease

semolina to dust

beaten egg to glaze

coarse salt flakes to sprinkle

1 Put all the dough ingredients except the olives and Parmesan into the bread-maker bucket with 300ml (½ pint) water, following the order and method specified in the manual.

2 Fit the bucket into the bread maker and set to the dough programme with raisin setting, if applicable. Press start. Add the olives and Parmesan when the machine beeps, or halfway through the kneading cycle. Lightly oil two large baking sheets and sprinkle with semolina.

3 Once the dough is ready, turn out on to a worksurface and punch it down to deflate. Cover with a teatowel and leave to rest for 10 minutes.

4 Lightly flour a work surface and roll out the dough to a 30.5 × 20.5cm (12 × 8 in) rectangle, cover loosely with a teatowel and leave for 30 minutes until well risen.

5 Preheat the oven to 220°C (200°C fan oven) mark 7. Cut the dough

SAVE EFFORT

For convenience, make them several days in advance and store in an airtight tin. To serve, pop them into a moderate oven for a couple of minutes if they have softened slightly.

Makes 32

across the width into four thick bands. From each of these, cut eight very thin strips and transfer them to the baking sheet, stretching each one until it is about 28cm (11in) long, and spacing the strips 1cm (½in) apart.

6 Brush very lightly with beaten egg and sprinkle with salt flakes. Bake for 18–20 minutes until crisp and golden. Transfer the grissini to a wire rack to cool.

Cheese Straws

Hands-on time: 10 minutes, plus chilling
Cooking time: about 20 minutes, plus cooling

200g (7oz) self-raising flour, sifted, plus extra to dust
a pinch of cayenne pepper
125g (4oz) unsalted butter, diced and chilled, plus extra to grease
125g (4oz) Parmesan, finely grated
2 medium eggs
1 tsp ready-made English mustard
sesame and poppy seeds to sprinkle

1 Put the flour, cayenne and butter into a food processor and pulse until the mixture resembles breadcrumbs. (Alternatively, rub the butter into the flour and cayenne in a large bowl by hand, until it resembles fine crumbs.) Add the Parmesan and mix in.

2 Crack one egg into a bowl. Separate the other egg, put the white to one side and add the egg yolk to the bowl with the whole egg. Mix in the mustard. Add to the flour mixture and mix together. Lightly flour a board, tip the mixture on to the board and knead lightly for 30 seconds, then wrap in clingfilm and chill in the fridge for 30 minutes.

3 Preheat the oven to 180°C (160°C fan oven) mark 4. Grease two baking sheets. Roll out the pastry on a lightly floured worksurface to a 23 x 30.5cm (9 x 12in) rectangle, cut out 24 straws and carefully twist each straw twice. Put on the baking sheets.

4 Beat the reserved egg white with a fork until frothy, and brush over the cheese straws, then sprinkle with the sesame and poppy seeds. Bake for 18–20 minutes until golden. Remove from the oven and cool for 5 minutes, then transfer to a wire rack and leave to cool completely.

Makes 24

Herb Vinegar

To make 600ml (1 pint), you will need:
25g (1oz) fresh herbs, plus extra sprigs for bottling, 600ml (1 pint) red or white wine vinegar.

1 Put the herbs and vinegar into a pan and bring to the boil. Pour into a heatproof bowl, cover and leave to soak overnight.
2 Strain through a muslin-lined sieve and bottle with herb sprigs. Store for one week before using.

Garlic, Soy and Honey

To make about 100ml (3½fl oz), you will need:
1 garlic clove, crushed, 2 tsp each soy sauce and honey, 1 tbsp cider vinegar, 4 tbsp olive oil, freshly ground black pepper.

1 Put the garlic in a small bowl. Add the soy sauce, honey, vinegar and oil, season to taste with pepper and whisk together thoroughly.
2 If not using, store in a cool place and whisk briefly before using.

Lemon Vinaigrette

To make about 150ml (¼ pint), you will need:
2 tbsp lemon juice, 2 tsp runny honey, 8 tbsp extra virgin olive oil, 3 tbsp freshly chopped mint, 4 tbsp roughly chopped flat-leafed parsley, salt and freshly ground black pepper.

1 Put the lemon juice, honey and seasoning to taste in a bowl and whisk to combine. Gradually whisk in the oil and stir in the herbs.
2 If not using immediately, store in a cool place and whisk before using.

Sun-dried Tomato

To make about 100ml (3½fl oz), you will need:

2 sun-dried tomatoes in oil, drained, 2 tbsp oil from sun-dried tomato jar, 2 tbsp red wine vinegar, 1 garlic clove, 1 tbsp sun-dried tomato paste, a pinch of sugar (optional), 2 tbsp extra virgin olive oil, salt and freshly ground black pepper.

1   Put the sun-dried tomatoes and oil, the vinegar, garlic and tomato paste into a blender or food processor. Add the sugar, if you like.
2   With the motor running, pour the oil through the feeder tube and whiz briefly to make a fairly thick dressing. Season to taste with salt and ground black pepper.
3   If not using store in a cool place and whisk briefly before using.

Fruit Vinegar

To make 600ml (1 pint), you will need:

450g (1lb) raspberries and blackberries, plus extra for bottling, 600ml (1 pint) red wine vinegar.

1   Put the fruit into a bowl and, using the back of a spoon, break it up, then add the vinegar. Cover and leave to stand for three days, stirring now and then.
2   Strain through a muslin-lined sieve and bottle with extra fruits. Store for two weeks before using.

Dazzling Canapés

Easy Ways To Plan Your Party

Use this handy guide to help you plan the perfect event.

Entertaining

Plan ahead and you are more likely to enjoy the occasion. Avoid planning a meal that is too complicated, and don't tackle a recipe that is totally unfamiliar – or have a practice run first. When deciding on a menu, keep it as well balanced as possible. Think about the colours, flavours and textures of the foods – rich and light, sweet and savoury, crunchy and smooth, hot and cold. Don't have cream or fruit featuring in all the courses; avoid an all-brown menu.

Select produce in season, for the best flavour and value for money. Check whether any of your guests have special dietary needs and plan appropriately. Try to cook an entirely meatless meal even if there is going to be just one vegetarian – it's not as difficult as it sounds, and rarely does anybody notice!

It is worthwhile choosing dishes that can be prepared well ahead of time or prepared up to a certain point, only needing a little last-minute finishing in the kitchen.

Planning the event

Make a master shopping list and separate lists of dishes to be prepared ahead, with a note of when to make them. Plan fridge and freezer space; for a large party, you may need to make different arrangements such as asking your neighbour to keep some foods in their fridge, or putting bulky items into cool boxes. Check that you have candles if you plan to use them.

Make invitations to a dinner party over the phone about 10–12 days in advance. Mention whether it's a formal or informal occasion, the date and time, address if necessary, and say if there are any special dress requirements to avoid embarrassing situations! If you are sending written invitations, post them two to three weeks in advance.

Check that table linen is laundered and ironed ahead of time, and that glasses and cutlery are clean. Clean the house a day or two beforehand. Buy or order wine and drinks in advance and avoid doing all the shopping at once.

Handy hints for entertaining

Try to strike a good balance between hot and cold items, as well as light and substantial ones. Most supermarkets have a good selection of ready-to-eat or cook appetisers, if you haven't time to make some. You can also use good-quality bought ingredients, such as mayonnaise and fresh sauces, to save time.

- A freezer is invaluable when entertaining, whether on a grand scale or just dinner for two.
- Keep a supply of ready-to-bake bread in the fridge or freezer for quick fresh bread. Freeze packs of half-baked breads to pop in the oven as and when needed.
- Keep a supply of luxury ice cream in the freezer.
- Remember to unwrap cheeses and bring them to room temperature at least an hour before serving, keeping them lightly covered, to prevent drying out, until the last minute.
- Make ice well in advance.
- During the winter, if you run out of fridge space, use a greenhouse or garage to keep drinks and other perishables cold.
- Use the microwave to reheat pre-cooked vegetables, sauces and gravy.
- Decide in advance where you are going to stack dirty plates. A kitchen overflowing with washing-up looks unsightly, so consider paying someone to do this for you on the day.

Spicy Nuts

Hands-on time: 10 minutes
Cooking time: about 20 minutes, plus cooling

450g (1lb) mixed unsalted nuts and
seeds, such as hazelnuts, peanuts,
cashews, macadamias, Brazil nuts,
pumpkin and sunflower seeds
2 tbsp olive oil
1–2 red chillies, seeded and
finely chopped (see Safety Tip)
1½ tbsp fresh thyme leaves
2 garlic cloves, finely chopped
1¼ tsp rock salt
freshly ground black pepper

1 Preheat the oven to 200°C (180°C fan
oven) mark 6. Mix together all the
ingredients in a large bowl with the
rock salt and lots of pepper.
2 Put the nut mixture on a baking
sheet and roast for 15–20 minutes,
tossing occasionally, until the nuts
are golden. Leave to cool completely,
then empty into bowls and serve.

SAVE EFFORT

Complete the recipe up to a week
in advance. Cool, then transfer to
an airtight container and store at
room temperature.

SAFETY TIP
Chillies can be quite mild to
blisteringly hot, depending on the
type of chilli and its ripeness. Taste
a small piece first to check it's not
too hot for you. Be extremely careful
when handling chillies not to touch
or rub your eyes with your fingers,
or they will sting. Wash knives
immediately after handling chillies.
As a precaution, use rubber gloves
when preparing them, if you like.

Makes 450g (1lb)

Poppadom Scoops

Hands-on time: 10 minutes

¼ red onion, finely chopped
1 ripe mango, peeled, stoned and
   finely diced
½ green chilli, seeded and
   finely chopped (see Safety Tip,
   page 38)
a small handful of fresh coriander,
   finely chopped
grated zest and juice of 1 lime
20 mini poppadoms
salt and freshly ground black pepper

SAVE TIME

Complete the recipe up the end
of step 1 one day in advance, but
don't add the coriander. Cover
and chill in the fridge, then
complete the recipe up to 1 hour
before serving.

1 Mix the onion, mango, chilli,
   coriander, lime zest and juice and
   some seasoning together in a
   medium bowl.
2 Spoon into poppadoms and serve.

Mini Eggs Benedict

Hands-on time: 20 minutes
Cooking time: about 5 minutes

oil to grease
12 quail eggs
3 standard thin-cut white bread slices
1 tbsp mayonnaise or jar of
 ready-made hollandaise
2–3 ham slices
freshly ground black pepper

1 Bring a medium pan quarter-filled with water to a simmer. Grease a lipped baking tray, then put the tray on top of the pan to heat up. Carefully crack all the quail eggs into a bowl, then gently pour the eggs on to the hot tray, moving the yolks so they are not touching one another. The steam will cook the eggs in 3–5 minutes.

2 Meanwhile, toast the bread slices. Use a 3.5cm (1½in) round cutter to stamp out 12 circles of toast. Top each circle with a dab of mayonnaise or hollandaise. Next, stamp out ham circles with the same cutter and put one circle on each toast stack.

3 When the egg whites are cooked (and the yolks are still soft), lift the tray off the steam. Use the cutter to stamp around each yolk and use a palette knife to transfer the egg circles to the stacks. Crack over some black pepper and serve.

SAVE TIME

These mini eggs are best made fresh, but will sit happily for up to 30 minutes once assembled.

Makes 12

Scotch Quail Eggs

Hands-on time: 25 minutes
Cooking time: about 20 minutes

300g (11oz) Cumberland pork
  sausages, about 5
flour to dust
1 large egg, lightly beaten
75g (3oz) dried breadcrumbs
12 hard-boiled quail eggs
2–3 tbsp vegetable oil to fry
sea salt and mustard to serve

1 Preheat the oven to 200°C (180°C
fan oven) mark 6. Squeeze the
sausage meat out of their skins into
a bowl. Discard the skins. Put some
flour, the egg and breadcrumbs into
separate small bowls.

2 Divide the meat into twelve equal
portions. With lightly floured hands,
form a portion into a flat patty about
6.5cm (2½in) across in the palm
of one hand. Put a boiled quail
egg in the middle, then shape the
meat around it. Put to one side
on a board and repeat with the
remaining eggs and meat.

3 Dip the covered eggs in the flour,
tap off excess, then dip in the beaten
egg, and coat in the breadcrumbs.

4 Heat the oil in a large frying pan
over a medium-high heat. Add
the coated eggs and fry, turning
regularly, until golden on each side
(in batches if necessary). Transfer
to a baking tray.

5 Cook the eggs in the oven for 10
minutes. Serve warm or at room
temperature (sliced in half, if you
like) with sea salt and mustard.

SAVE EFFORT

Hard-boil quail eggs up to two
days ahead. Cool, shell, cover and
chill. Complete the recipe up to a
day ahead (if needed). Cool and
chill. Allow to come up to room
temperature, or warm in a 180°C
(160°C fan oven) mark 4 oven for
5–10 minutes, before serving.

Makes 12

Mini Jacket Potatoes

Hands-on time: 20 minutes
Cooking time: about 40 minutes

20 baby new potatoes
1 tbsp oil
100g (3½oz) crème fraîche
finely grated zest and juice of 1 lemon
1 tbsp freshly chopped dill, plus extra
  to garnish
100g (3½oz) smoked salmon strips
lumpfish caviar
salt and freshly ground black pepper

1 Preheat the oven to 200°C (180°C fan oven) mark 6. Put the potatoes in a roasting tin and toss through the oil and plenty of seasoning. Roast for 35–40 minutes until golden and tender. Leave to cool to room temperature.

2 In a small bowl, stir together the crème fraîche, lemon zest and juice, dill and seasoning.

3 Cut a slit down the length of a potato, then pull the sides apart a little to open. Repeat with remaining potatoes. Top each with a dollop of the crème fraîche mixture, a curl of salmon, a few caviar eggs and a dill frond. Serve.

Makes 20

Loaded Potato Skins

Hands-on time: 15 minutes
Cooking time: about 1½ hours, plus cooling

4 baking potatoes
½ tbsp wholegrain mustard
1 tbsp freshly chopped chives
75g (3oz) red Leicester or mature
   Cheddar, grated
4 tbsp soured cream
2 medium egg yolks
1 tbsp olive oil
salt and freshly ground black pepper
tomato ketchup and barbecue sauce to
   serve (optional)

1 Preheat the oven to 200°C (180°C
   fan oven) mark 6. Prick each potato
   a few times with a fork and roast for
   1-1¼ hours or until the potato can
   be easily pierced with a knife. Leave
   until cool enough to handle.

2 Carefully halve each potato, then
   cut each half into three long wedges.
   Scoop most of the flesh into a bowl
   (leaving just enough attached to the
   skin to maintain its shape). Arrange
   the wedges skin-side down on a
   large baking tray.

3 To the potato flesh, add the mustard,
   chopped chives, grated cheese,
   soured cream, egg yolks, oil and
   plenty of seasoning.

4 Load the filling on to the skins and
   bake in the oven for about 15–20
   minutes or until golden. Leave
   the wedges to cool for at least 10
   minutes before serving on their
   own, or with tomato ketchup or
   barbecue sauce.

SAVE EFFORT

Prepare and fill the potato skins
up to 4 hours ahead. Cover and
chill. To serve, uncover and
complete the recipe.

Makes 24

Thai Crab Mayo Croustades

Hands-on time: 15 minutes

100g (3½oz) white crab meat

1½ tsp fish sauce

2½ tbsp mayonnaise

½–1 red chilli, seeded and
   finely chopped (see Safety Tip,
   page 38)

a small handful of fresh coriander,
   chopped, plus extra to garnish
   (optional)

15 mini croustade cases

salt and freshly ground black pepper

SAVE TIME

Make the crab mixture up to
a day ahead but don't add the
coriander. Cover and chill.
Complete the recipe to serve.

1   In a medium bowl, stir together
the first five ingredients. Check the
seasoning and adjust to taste. Fill
each croustade case with a spoonful
of the crab mixture, then garnish
with extra coriander, if you like.

Makes 15

Party Prawns

Hands-on time: 10 minutes
Cooking time: about 5 minutes

5–7 rashers streaky bacon
150g pack raw king prawns
25g (1oz) butter
1 tbsp chopped fresh chives
freshly ground black pepper

1 Slice each bacon rasher in half lengthways, then in half widthways. Wrap a bacon strip around the middle of each raw prawn.

2 Heat the butter in a large frying pan. Add the prawns and cook for 3–5 minutes until the prawns are bright pink and bacon is cooked.

3 Season well with ground black pepper and sprinkle over the chives. Serve immediately with cocktail sticks.

SAVE EFFORT

Complete the recipe to the end of step 1 up to 4 hours in advance. Cover and keep in the fridge, then complete the recipe to serve.

Smoked Fish Bites

Hands-on time: 15 minutes

100g (3½oz) full-fat cream cheese
100g (3½oz) skinned smoked fish,
   such as mackerel
finely grated zest of 1 lemon
3 rye bread slices, about 150g (5oz)
1 tbsp fresh chopped chives
salt and freshly ground black pepper

SAVE TIME

Assemble the canapés up to 4
hours ahead, cover and keep in
the fridge. Alternatively, prepare
to the end of step 1 up to two days
ahead. Cover and chill the mixture.
Complete the recipe to serve.

1 Put the cream cheese into a food
processor. Add the skinned smoked
fish, lemon zest and some seasoning.
Pulse briefly until well combined
but still with some texture. Empty
into a bowl.

2 Cut each slice of rye bread into nine
equal pieces. Use a knife to smear
some fish pâté on to each piece of
bread. Garnish with freshly cracked
black pepper and chives.

Makes 27

Sweet Onion Sausage Rolls

Hands-on time: 20 minutes, plus chilling
Cooking time: about 15 minutes

300g (11oz) sausage meat
a small handful of fresh parsley,
    finely chopped
375g pack ready-rolled shortcrust
    pastry (in a rectangular sheet)
2 tbsp onion marmalade (bought)
1 large egg, lightly beaten
poppy seeds to sprinkle

1 Put the sausage meat into a large
   bowl; stir in the parsley. Unroll the
   pastry sheet and cut lengthways
   into four equal strips. Thinly spread
   1 tbsp of the onion marmalade
   lengthways down the middle of
   one of the strips. Repeat with one
   other strip.

2 Divide the sausage mixture in half.
   Shape one half into a thin cylinder
   as long as the pastry strips, then
   position it on top of one of the
   marmalade strips. Repeat with
   the remaining sausage mixture.
   Brush the visible pastry around the
   sausage cylinders with beaten egg,
   then top with the remaining pastry
   strips. Press down on the edges to
   seal. Transfer to a baking sheet and
   chill for 30 minutes.

3 Preheat the oven to 200°C (180°C
   fan oven) mark 6. Line two baking
   trays with baking parchment. Brush
   both rolls with egg and sprinkle
   over some poppy seeds. Cut into
   4cm (1½in) pieces and place on the
   prepared trays. Cook for 15 minutes
   or until golden. Serve warm or at
   room temperature.

SAVE TIME

Complete up to end of step 2 up
to one day ahead. Cover and chill.
Complete the recipe to serve.

Makes about 22

Mini Hotdogs

Hands-on time: 25 minutes, plus chilling
Cooking time: about 40 minutes

1 tbsp vegetable oil
1 onion, thinly sliced
375g sheet ready-rolled
   shortcrust pastry
flour, to dust
24 raw cocktail sausages
1 medium egg, lightly beaten
French's mustard and tomato ketchup
   to serve

1 Heat the oil in a frying pan and gently cook the onion for 10 minutes or until softened but not coloured.

2 Unroll the pastry sheet on to a lightly floured worksurface and trim the edges to neaten. Cut out 24 squares, each measuring 6cm (2½in). Put a pinch of onion in a line down the middle of each square and top with a sausage (laid straight or diagonally across the pastry). Lift the empty pastry up and stick to the sides of the sausage. Transfer to a baking sheet. Complete with the remaining pastry, onion and sausages. Brush the hot dogs all over with beaten egg and chill in the fridge for 10 minutes.

3 Preheat the oven to 200°C (180°C fan oven) mark 6. Cook the hotdogs in the oven for 25–30 minutes until golden. Leave to cool for 5 minutes. Serve warm or at room temperature with a squeeze of French's mustard or tomato ketchup.

SAVE TIME

Make the hot dogs to the end of step 2 up to one day ahead. Loosely cover and chill. To serve, brush with more beaten egg and complete the recipe.

58

Makes 24

Harissa Chicken Balls with Yogurt Dip

Hands-on time: 20 minutes
Cooking time: about 25 minutes

2 skinless chicken breasts
1½–2 tsp rose harissa paste, to taste
finely grated zest of
½ a medium orange
2 spring onions
2 tbsp olive oil
salt and freshly ground black pepper

For the dip

100g (3½oz) natural yogurt
few fresh mint leaves, finely sliced
5cm (2in) cucumber, grated

SAVE TIME

Cook the chicken balls up to a
day ahead. Cool, cover and chill.
Make dip up to 3 hours ahead.
Chill. To serve, reheat the chicken
balls in an oven preheated to
160°C (140°C fan oven) mark 3
for 10 minutes. Stir the dip before
serving.

1 Put the chicken, harissa, orange zest and some seasoning into a food processor. Snip in the spring onions, then whiz until fairly smooth. Remove the blade and shape the mixture into bite-size balls.

2 Heat the oil over a medium heat in a large non-stick frying pan. Add the meatballs (you will need to do this in batches) and fry for 10–12 minutes, turning frequently, until golden and cooked through (check by cutting into one). Put to one side.

3 To make the dip, mix all the ingredients together with some seasoning and put into a small serving bowl. Serve the chicken balls warm or at room temperature with the dip on the side.

Makes about 28

Tangerine Jelly Shots

Hands-on time: 10 minutes, plus chilling
Cooking time: about 3 minutes

5 gelatine leaves
12 tangerines, about 1kg (2lb 2oz)
150g (5oz) caster sugar
double cream, to serve (optional)

1 Put the gelatine in a bowl and cover with cold water. Leave to soak for 5 minutes. Meanwhile zest 2 tangerines and put the zest into a large pan. Squeeze the juice from the zested and whole tangerines and add to the pan with the sugar.

2 Lift the gelatine out of the water (discard the water) and add to the pan. Heat gently until the sugar dissolves. Strain the mixture into a large jug with a good pouring spout and make up to 1 litre (1¾ pints) with cold water. Pour the mixture into 12 small glasses and chill in the fridge for at least 5 hours, preferably overnight.

3 To serve, take the jellies out of fridge 5 minutes before you need them to allow to soften slightly. Serve with spoons and topped with double cream, if you like.

SAVE EFFORT

Make these delicious jellies up to two days ahead.

Makes 12

Perfect Catering

The table below shows approximate quantities to serve 12 people. For 25, multiply the quantities by 2; and for 50, multiply by 4. When dealing with larger numbers, for 75, multiply by 5½ and for 100, multiply by 7.

Starters	
Soups	2.6 litres (4½ pints)
Pâtés	1.1kg (2½lb)
Smoked salmon	900g (2lb)
Prawns	900g (2lb)
Main dishes	
Boneless chicken or turkey	1.8kg (4lb)
Whole chicken	three 1.4kg (3lb) oven-ready birds
Turkey	one 5.4kg (12lb) oven-ready bird

Lamb/beef/pork	
Boneless	2–2.3kg (4½–5lb)
On the bone	3.2–3.6kg (7–8lb)
Mince	2kg (4½lb)
Fish	
Whole with head	2.3kg (5lb)
Steaks	twelve 175g (6oz) steaks
Fillets	2kg (4½lb)
Prawns (main course)	1.4kg (3lb)
Turkey	
6–10 people	2.3–3.6kg (5–8lb)
10–15	3.6–5kg (8–11lb)
15–20	5–6.8kg (11–15lb)

Accompaniments	
Roast and mashed potatoes	2kg (4½lb)
New potatoes	1.8kg (4lb)
Rice and pasta	700g (1½lb)
Green vegetables	1.4kg (3lb)
Fresh spinach	3.6kg (8lb)

Salads	
Tomatoes	700g (1½lb)
Salad leaves	2 medium heads
Cucumber	1 large
French dressing	175ml (6fl oz) 300ml (½ pint)

Bread	
Fresh uncut bread	1 large loaf
Medium sliced loaf	1 large (approximately 24 slices)

Cheese	
For a cheese and wine party	1.4kg (3lb)
To serve at the end of a meal	700g (1½lb)

Butter	
To serve with bread or biscuits and cheese	225g (8oz)
To serve with bread and biscuits and cheese	350g (12oz)
For sandwiches	175g (6oz) softened butter for 12 rounds

Cream	
For pudding	600ml (1 pint) single cream
For coffee	300ml (½ pint)

Coffee and tea	
Ground coffee	125g (4oz) for 12 medium cups
Instant	75g (3oz) for 12 large cups
Milk	allow 450ml (¾ pint) for 12 cups of tea

Afternoon
Tea Party

Perfect Sandwiches and Dips

Party sandwiches don't have to be dull. All you need is a little imagination and lots of delicious fillings.

Aim for variety

There are all sorts of interesting breads and rolls available that are perfect for perking up sandwiches.

- Children love miniature versions of grown-up food; hearty sandwiches may put them off tucking in.
- Look out for mini wholemeal pittas and dinner rolls.
- Flavoured wraps are a quick and easy way to make sandwiches for large numbers and cost-effective too – once filled and rolled they can be sliced into bite-size pieces.
- Sliced bread can be transformed into fun shapes with cookie cutters – try heart or star-shaped sandwiches for the party princess, farmyard animals or dinosaurs and even cars. Use the same shaped cutter to cut out slices of cheese or ham for a neat fit.
- Arrange alternate sandwich squares made with white and wholemeal bread to make a draughts board.

Save time

- Chilling a loaf will make it easier to cut.
- Don't forget to soften the butter to make it easier to spread.
- Fillings can be made a day ahead, covered and stored in the fridge until you are ready to assemble the sandwiches.
- Rolls and sandwiches can be made up to 3 hours ahead. Cover with a slightly damp teatowel, then foil or clingfilm, and store in the fridge.
- Prepare a few plain buttered rolls for fussy eaters.

Quick and easy fillings

Each of the following recipes will make enough filling for three rounds of sliced bread sandwiches.

Egg mayonnaise

Put 3 medium eggs in a small pan and cover with water. Bring to the boil and cook for 6 minutes. Drain and run them under cold water. Shell, then mash the eggs with 2 tbsp mayonnaise. Stir in mustard and cress.

Tuna and sweetcorn

Mix together a 185g can tuna in spring water with a 200g can sweetcorn, drained, and 2 tbsp mayonnaise.

Chunky houmous

Mix together a 200g tub houmous with ¼ cucumber, chopped, and 4 medium tomatoes, seeded and chopped.

Two-cheese and spring onion

Grate 100g (3½oz) mild Cheddar and 100g (3½oz) red Leicester into a bowl. Stir in 4 finely chopped spring onions and 1 tbsp mayonnaise.

Quick and easy dips

Arrange a variety of dips with a pile of tempting, colourful vegetables such as carrot, celery and cucumber sticks, slices of different coloured pepper and cherry tomatoes.

Cherry tomato and pesto

Roughly chop 6 cherry tomatoes and stir into a tub of fresh pesto with 2 tbsp natural yogurt.

Cucumber and yogurt

Seed and chop ¼ cucumber and put into a bowl with 1 tbsp freshly chopped mint. Stir in 150g (5oz) Greek yogurt.

Herby cheese

Beat together 300g (11oz) herbed cream cheese with 4 tbsp mayonnaise and 2 tbsp freshly chopped parsley.

Deluxe Carrot Cake

Hands-on time: 30 minutes
Cooking time: about 1¾ hours, plus cooling

225ml (8fl oz) sunflower oil, plus extra
   to grease
225g (8oz) light muscovado sugar
4 medium eggs
225g (8oz) self-raising flour
1 tsp bicarbonate of soda
1½ tsp each mixed spice and
   ground cinnamon
1 orange
150g (5oz) sultanas
200g (7oz) carrots, peeled and
   coarsely grated
50g (2oz) walnuts, chopped
50g (2oz) preserved stem ginger,
   drained and chopped

For the frosting and decoration

600g (1lb 5oz) cream cheese
200g (7oz) icing sugar, sifted
finely grated zest of 1 orange
marzipan carrots (see opposite)

1 Preheat the oven to 170°C (150°C fan oven) mark 3. Grease the base and sides of a 20.5cm (8in) cake tin and line with baking parchment.

2 Whisk the oil, sugar and eggs in a large bowl until smooth. Stir in the flour, bicarbonate of soda and spices. Finely grate the zest of the orange and add to the mixture with the juice from only half the orange. Add the sultanas, carrots, walnuts and ginger and mix well. Spoon the mixture into the prepared tin.

3 Bake for 30 minutes, then cover the top of the cake loosely with foil and bake for a further 1¼ hours or until a skewer inserted into the centre comes out clean. Leave to cool in the tin for 5 minutes, then turn out on to a wire rack (leave the lining paper on) and leave to cool completely.

4 When the cake is cold, peel off the lining paper and cut the cake in two horizontally.

Cuts into 12 slices

5 To make the frosting, mix the cream cheese, icing sugar and orange zest in a bowl. Use half the frosting to sandwich the two cake halves together. Spread the remaining frosting over the top and decorate with marzipan carrots.

To make marzipan carrots
Colour 75g (3oz) marzipan with orange food colouring and 15g (½oz) with green food colouring. Divide the orange marzipan into 12 pieces and shape them into cones. Mark on ridges with a cocktail stick. Split the green marzipan into 12, then shape into leaf-like fronds and stick to the carrot tops.

The Golden Rules

Cake recipes vary greatly, not only by the methods used to make the cakes, but also in the balance of the various ingredients. There are no secrets to making a great cake – all you need to do is follow these simple golden rules.

- If making larger cakes, check first that your oven is big enough. There should be at least 5cm (2in) oven space all around the cake tin to ensure that it cooks evenly.
- Always make sure you have the correct tin shape and size according to the recipe you are making. The tin sizes quoted in this book refer to the base measurement of the tin.
- Ensure the tin is properly prepared and lined for baking the recipe you have chosen to make.
- Check that you have all the necessary ingredients stated in the recipe and that they are at the correct temperature.
- Weigh out and/or measure all the ingredients accurately using scales, measuring spoons and a measuring jug. Always work in either metric or imperial.
- Use the egg sizes stated in the recipe. Substituting different sizes can affect the balance of the cake mixture.
- Sifting dry ingredients together helps not only to aerate, but also to disperse lumps.
- Store flours and raising agents in well-sealed packets or airtight containers in a cool, dry place.
- When making cakes by hand, beat well with a wooden spoon until the mixture is light and fluffy (only possible if your butter is at the correct temperature).
- Be careful not to over-process or over-beat the mixture; the mixture can over-rise in the oven, then collapse and dip in the centre during baking.

- If ingredients have to be folded into a cake mixture, use a large metal spoon, which will cut cleanly through the mixture. Keep scooping down to the bottom of the bowl, then turning the mixture on top of itself, while at the same time giving the bowl a quarter twist. Continue just up until the ingredients are combined – do not be tempted to over-fold the cake mixture. Try not to be heavy-handed when folding in flour.
- Don't let a cake mixture sit around once you've made it: pop it straight into the cake tin and into the oven, otherwise the raising agents will start to react.
- Before any baking, check the temperature of your oven is correct by investing in an inexpensive oven thermometer.
- Check your oven is preheated to the correct temperature stated in the recipe. Once the cake is in the oven, resist the temptation to open the oven door before at least three-quarters of the specified baking time has passed – the heat will escape and the cake will sink.
- If your cake appears to be browning too quickly, cover the top loosely with foil or greaseproof paper towards the end of cooking.
- If conditions are cold, the mixture will take longer to cook. Similarly, if it is a very hot day, then baking will be slightly quicker.
- Always check the cake is cooked 5–10 minutes before the given baking time, just in case the oven is a little fast.
- After it has come out of the oven, leave the cake to cool in the tin for the specified time then turn out on to a wire rack to cool completely.
- Let the tins cool completely before washing them in warm, soapy water with a non-abrasive sponge.

Genoese Sponge

Hands-on time: 25 minutes
Cooking time: about 30 minutes or about 40 minutes, plus cooling

40g (1½oz) unsalted butter, plus extra
  to grease

65g (2½oz) plain flour, plus extra to
  dust

3 large eggs

75g (3oz) caster sugar

1 tbsp cornflour

For the filling and topping

3–4 tbsp strawberry, raspberry or
  apricot jam

125ml (4fl oz) whipping cream,
  whipped (optional)

icing sugar or caster sugar

1 Grease two 18cm (7in) sandwich tins
or one deep 18cm (7in) round cake
tin, base-line with greaseproof paper
and dust the sides with a little flour.

2 Put the butter into a small pan and
heat gently to melt, then take off
the heat and leave to stand for a few
minutes to cool slightly.

3 Put the eggs and sugar into a bowl
and, using a hand-held electric
whisk, beat until well blended. Place
the bowl over a pan of hot water,
making sure the base of the bowl
doesn't touch the water, and whisk
until the mixture is pale and creamy
and thick enough to leave a trail on
the surface when the whisk is lifted
– this should take about 5 minutes.
Remove the bowl from the pan and
whisk until cool.

4 Preheat the oven to 180°C (160°C fan
oven) mark 4. Sift the plain flour
and cornflour into the egg bowl,
then use a large metal spoon to
carefully fold in (trying to knock
out as little air as possible).

5 Pour the melted and cooled butter
around the edges of the mixture,
leaving any butter sediment behind
in the pan. Very lightly, fold in the
butter until it has been incorporated
into the mixture. Pour into the
prepared tin(s).

6 Bake the cake(s) on the middle shelf
of the oven for 25–30 minutes for

Cuts into 6 large slices

the sandwich tins, or 35–40 minutes for the deep tin, until well risen and springy to the touch when lightly pressed in the centre. Loosen the edges with a palette knife and leave to cool in the tin(s) for 10 minutes. Turn out on to a wire rack (leave the lining paper on) and leave to cool completely.

7 When the cake(s) is cold, peel off the lining paper (and halve the single cake horizontally) and sandwich the two cakes/halves together with jam and whipped cream, if you like. Dust with icing sugar, or sprinkle the top with caster sugar. Serve in slices.

Cappuccino and Walnut Cake

Hands-on time: 30 minutes
Cooking time: about 35 minutes, plus cooling

65g (2½oz) unsalted butter, melted and cooled, plus extra to grease
100g (3½oz) plain flour
1 tsp baking powder
4 medium eggs
125g (4oz) caster sugar
1 tbsp chicory and coffee essence
75g (3oz) walnuts, toasted, cooled and finely chopped

For the decoration

50g (2oz) walnuts
1 tbsp granulated sugar
¼ tsp ground cinnamon
fresh unsprayed violets to decorate (optional)

For the icing

200g (7oz) white chocolate, chopped
4 tsp chicory and coffee essence
2 × 250g tubs mascarpone

1 Preheat the oven to 190°C (170°C fan oven) mark 5. Grease two 20.5 × 4cm (8 × 1½in) round cake tins and base-line each with a circle of greased greaseproof paper.

2 Sift the flour and baking powder together twice.

3 Using a hand-held electric whisk, beat the eggs and caster sugar in a large heatproof bowl set over a pan of barely simmering water for 3–4 minutes until light, thick and fluffy. Take the bowl off the heat and continue whisking until the mixture has cooled and the whisk leaves a ribbon trail for 8 seconds when lifted out of the bowl.

4 Fold in the butter, coffee essence and chopped walnuts. Sift half the flour into the mixture and, using a metal spoon, fold it in carefully but quickly. Sift and fold in the rest of the flour, taking care to knock out as little air as possible. Divide the mixture evenly between the

prepared tins and tap them lightly on the worksurface.

5 Bake for 20–25 minutes until the cakes spring back when lightly pressed in the centre. Leave to cool in the tins for 10 minutes, then turn out on to a wire rack (leave the lining paper on) and leave to cool completely. When the cakes are cold, peel off the lining paper.

6 To make the decoration, whiz the walnuts with the granulated sugar and cinnamon in a food processor or blender until finely chopped. Take care not to over-process the nuts or they'll become oily. ut to one side.

7 To make the icing, melt the chocolate slowly without stirring in a heatproof bowl set over a pan of gently simmering water, making sure the base of the bowl doesn't touch the water. In another bowl, add the coffee essence to the mascarpone and beat until smooth, then slowly beat in the chocolate.

Cuts into 10 slices

8 Spread one-third of the icing on top of one cake, then sandwich with the other cake. Smooth the remaining icing over the top and sides. Lift the cake on to a large piece of greaseproof paper and scatter the chopped nuts all around it, then lift the greaseproof up to press the nuts on to the sides. Transfer to a plate and decorate with the violets, if you like. Serve in slices.

Test It, Store It

Ovens vary and the time given in the recipe might be too short or too long to correctly cook what you are baking. Therefore, always test to ensure a successful result.

Testing sponges

1. Gently press the centre of the sponge. It should feel springy. If it's a whisked cake, it should be just shrinking away from the sides of the tin.
2. If you have to put it back into the oven, close the door gently so that the vibrations don't cause the cake to sink in the centre.

Testing fruit cakes

1 To test if a fruit cake is cooked, insert a skewer into the centre of the cake, leave for a few moments, then pull it out. If it comes away clean, the cake is ready.
2 If any cake mixture sticks to the skewer, the cake is not quite done, so put the cake back in the oven for a few more minutes, then test again with a clean skewer.

Cooling cakes

Always follow the cooling instructions stated in the recipe. If certain cakes are left for too long in the tin, they will sweat. Most rich fruit cakes, on the other hand, should be left to cool completely in the tin to help them stabilise. Make sure all cakes are completely cool before icing or storing.

Storing cakes

With the exception of rich fruit cakes and gingerbread, most cakes are best enjoyed freshly baked. If storing is necessary, use a cake tin or large plastic container. Make sure that the cake is completely cold before you put it into the container. If you haven't a large enough container, wrap the cake in a double layer of greaseproof paper and over-wrap with foil. Avoid putting rich fruit cakes in direct contact with foil – the fruit may react with it. Never store a cake in the same tin as biscuits, as the biscuits will quickly soften.

Most cakes, particularly sponges, freeze well, but they are generally best frozen before filling and decorating. If freezing a finished gateau, open-freeze first, then pack in a rigid container.

Banana Cake

Gluten Free

🍴 **Hands-on time:** 20 minutes
Cooking time: about 1 hour, plus cooling

125g (4oz) unsalted butter, softened, plus extra to grease

125g (4oz) light muscovado sugar

2 large eggs, lightly beaten

50g (2oz) smooth apple sauce

3 very ripe bananas, about 375g (13oz) peeled weight, mashed

1½ tsp mixed spice

150g (5oz) gluten-free plain flour blend

1 tsp gluten-free baking powder

a pinch of salt

For the icing

75g (3oz) unsalted butter, softened

100g (3½oz) icing sugar, sifted

50g (2oz) light muscovado sugar

½ tbsp milk (optional)

dried banana chips to decorate (optional)

1 Preheat the oven to 180°C (160°C fan oven) mark 4. Grease the base and sides of a 900g (2lb) loaf tin and line with baking parchment.

2 Using a hand-held electric whisk, beat the butter and muscovado sugar in a large bowl until pale and creamy. Gradually whisk in the eggs, then the apple sauce. Stir in the bananas.

3 Sift the spice, flour, baking powder and salt into the bowl, then use a large metal spoon to fold in (the mixture may look a little curdled). Spoon the mixture into the prepared tin.

4 Bake for 50 minutes–1 hour until risen and a skewer inserted into the centre comes out clean. Leave to cool in the tin for 10 minutes, then turn out on to a wire rack (leave the lining paper on) and leave to cool completely. When the cake is cold, remove the lining paper and put the cake on a serving plate.

5 To make the icing, whisk together the butter and both sugars until smooth. If needed, add a little milk to loosen. Spread over the top of the cooled cake. Decorate with banana chips, if you like. Serve in slices.

Cuts into 8–10 slices

Sticky Gingerbread

Hands-on time: 20 minutes
Cooking time: 1 hour 15 minutes, plus cooling

125g (4oz) unsalted butter, plus extra
   to grease
125g (4oz) light muscovado sugar
75g (3oz) black treacle
200g (7oz) golden syrup
250g (9oz) plain flour
2 tsp ground mixed spice
65g (2½oz) preserved stem ginger,
   finely chopped
2 large eggs
100ml (3½fl oz) milk
1 tsp bicarbonate of soda
extra treacle or golden syrup to glaze
   (optional)

1 Put the butter, sugar, treacle and
golden syrup in a saucepan and heat
gently until the butter has melted.
Leave to cool for 5 minutes. Grease
and line the bread-maker bucket
with baking parchment, if specified
in the manual.

2 Sift the flour and mixed spice
together into a bowl. Add the syrup
mixture, chopped ginger, eggs and
milk and stir well until combined.

3 In a cup, mix the bicarbonate of soda
with 2 tbsp hot water, then add to the
bowl. Stir the mixture well and pour
into the bread-maker bucket.

4 Fit the bucket into the bread
maker and set to the cake or bake
only programme. Select 1 hour 10
minutes on the timer and choose a
light crust. Press start.

5 To check whether the cake is done,
pierce the centre with a skewer;
it should come out fairly clean.
If necessary, re-set the timer for
a little longer.

6 Remove the bucket from the
machine, leave the cake in it for
5 minutes, then turn out on to a wire
rack. Brush the top of the cake with
the treacle or syrup to glaze, if you
like, and leave to cool.

Cuts into 10 slices

Lemon Drizzle Loaf

Hands-on time: 20 minutes
Cooking time: about 50 minutes, plus cooling

175g (6oz) unsalted butter, softened, plus extra to grease

175g (6oz) caster sugar

4 medium eggs, lightly beaten

3 lemons

125g (4oz) self-raising flour, sifted

50g (2oz) ground almonds

75g (3oz) sugar cubes

1 Preheat the oven to 180°C (160°C fan oven) mark 4. Grease a 900g (2lb) loaf tin and line with baking parchment.

2 Put the butter and caster sugar into a large bowl and, using a hand-held electric whisk, cream together until pale and fluffy – this should take about 5 minutes. Gradually beat in the eggs, followed by the finely grated zest of 2 of the lemons and the juice of ½ a lemon. Fold the flour and ground almonds into the butter mixture, then spoon into the prepared tin.

3 Bake for 40–50 minutes until a skewer inserted into the centre comes out clean. Leave to cool in the tin for 10 minutes, then turn out, peel off the lining paper and leave to cool on a wire rack until just warm.

4 Meanwhile, put the sugar cubes into a small bowl with the juice of 1½ lemons and the pared zest of 1 lemon (you should have 1 un-juiced lemon left over). Soak for 5 minutes, then use the back of a spoon to roughly crush the cubes. Spoon over the warm cake and leave to cool completely before serving in slices.

SAVE TIME

Store in an airtight container. It will keep for up to four days.

84

Fruity Teacake

Gluten Free

Hands-on time: 20 minutes, plus soaking
Cooking time: 1 hour, plus cooling

150ml (¼ pint) hot black tea, made with 2 Earl Grey tea bags

200g (7oz) sultanas

75g (3oz) ready-to-eat dried figs, roughly chopped

75g (3oz) ready-to-eat dried prunes, roughly chopped

a little vegetable oil

125g (4oz) dark muscovado sugar

2 medium eggs, beaten

225g (8oz) gluten-free flour

2 tsp wheat-free baking powder

2 tsp ground mixed spice

butter to serve (optional)

1 Pour the tea into a bowl and add all the dried fruit. Leave to soak for 30 minutes.

2 Preheat the oven to 190°C (170°C fan oven) mark 5. Oil a 900g (2lb) loaf tin and base-line with greaseproof paper.

3 Beat the sugar and eggs together in a large bowl until pale and slightly thickened. Add the flour, baking powder, mixed spice and soaked dried fruit and tea, then mix together well. Spoon the mixture into the prepared tin and level the surface.

4 Bake on the middle shelf of the oven for 45 minutes–1 hour. Leave to cool completely in the tin. When the cake is cold, turn out and peel off the lining paper. Serve sliced, with a little butter if you like.

SAVE TIME

Wrap in clingfilm and store in an airtight container. It will keep for up to five days.

Cuts into 12 slices

Cake Troubleshooting

Use this handy guide to help you find out where and why things might have gone wrong with your cake baking.

The cake sinks in the middle

- The oven door was opened too soon.
- The cake was under-baked.
- The ingredients haven't been measured accurately.
- The wrong size cake tin may have been used.

The cake has a cracked, domed top

- The oven temperature was too hot.
- The cake was too near the top of the oven.
- Insufficient liquid was used.
- The baking tin was too small.
- Too much raising agent was used.

The cake has a dense texture

- The mixture curdled when the eggs were being added.
- Too much liquid was used.
- The mixture was over-folded.
- Too little raising agent was used or an ineffective raising agent that was past its 'use-by date' was used.

The fruit has sunk to the bottom

- The mixture was too soft to support the weight of the fruit. This is liable to happen if the fruit was too sticky or wet.

The cake edges are crunchy

- The baking tin was over-greased.

Battenberg Delight

Hands-on time: 35 minutes
Cooking time: about 35 minutes, plus cooling

175g (6oz) unsalted butter, softened, plus extra to grease

175g (6oz) caster sugar

3 large eggs, lightly beaten

200g (7oz) self-raising flour

25g (1oz) ground almonds

a few drops of almond extract

pink and yellow food colouring

3–4 tbsp lemon curd

icing sugar to dust

500g (1lb 2oz) marzipan

1 Preheat the oven to 180°C (160°C fan oven) mark 4. Grease a 20.5cm (8in) square, straight-sided roasting/brownie tin. Cut a rectangle of baking parchment that measures exactly 20.5 × 30.5cm (8 × 12in). Fold it in half (short end to short end), then make a fold 5cm (2in) wide down the length of the closed side, bending it both ways to mark a pleat. Open up the parchment, then pinch the pleat back together (so that it stands perpendicular to the rest of the parchment). Position the parchment in the bottom of the tin – it should line the bottom exactly and provide a 5cm (2in) divider down the middle.

2 Using a hand-held electric whisk, cream the butter and caster sugar together in a large bowl until pale and fluffy. Gradually beat in the eggs, then use a large metal spoon to fold in the flour, ground almonds and almond extract.

3 Spoon half the mixture into a separate bowl. Use the food colouring to tint one half yellow and the other pink. Spoon one batter into each side of the prepared tin, making sure the parchment doesn't shift, and level the surface.

4 Bake for 30–35 minutes until a skewer inserted into the centre of each side comes out clean. Leave to cool in the tin.

5 When the cake is cold, turn out of the tin and peel off the lining paper.

Using a bread knife, level the top of each cake and remove any browned sponge. Stack the cakes and trim the sides and ends to reveal coloured sponge. With the sponges still stacked, halve the cakes lengthways to make four equal strips of sponge.

6 Spread a thin layer of lemon curd along one long side of a yellow strip, then stick it to a long side of a pink strip. Repeat with the remaining two strips. Stick the pairs of sponges on top of one another with more curd to give a chequerboard effect, then trim to neaten. Spread the ends of the cake with more curd.

7 Lightly dust the worksurface with icing sugar, then roll out one-eighth of the marzipan until 5mm (¼in) thick. Stick to one end of the cake and trim with scissors. Repeat with the other end.

8 Roll out the remaining marzipan into a long strip, 5mm (¼in) thick – it needs to be at least 22cm (8½in)

Serves 10

wide and 35.5cm (14in) long. Brush with lemon curd. Place the cake on the marzipan at one of the short ends, then trim the width of the marzipan strip to match the cake. Roll the cake, sticking it to the marzipan as you go. Trim the end to neaten. Serve in slices.

Oven Scones

Hands-on time: 15 minutes
Cooking time: 10 minutes, plus cooling

40g (1½oz) unsalted butter, diced, plus extra to grease

225g (8oz) self-raising flour, plus extra to dust

a pinch of salt

1 tsp baking powder

about 150ml (¼ pint) milk

beaten egg or milk to glaze

whipped cream, or butter and jam to serve

1 Preheat the oven to 220°C (200°C fan oven) mark 7. Grease a baking sheet.

2 Sift the flour, salt and baking powder into a bowl. Rub in the butter until the mixture resembles fine breadcrumbs. Using a knife to stir it in, add enough milk to give a fairly soft dough.

3 Gently roll or pat out the dough on a lightly floured worksurface to a 2cm (¾in) thickness and then, using a 6.5cm (2½in) plain cutter, cut out rounds. Put on the prepared baking sheet and brush the tops with beaten egg or milk.

4 Bake for about 10 minutes until golden brown and well risen. Transfer to a wire rack and leave to cool.

5 Serve warm, split and filled with whipped cream, or spread with butter and jam.

SAVE EFFORT

To ensure a good rise, avoid heavy handling and make sure the rolled-out dough is at least 2cm (¾in) thick.

Makes 8

Perfect Coffee and Tea

Use this handy guide to help you find out how
much coffee and tea to serve at your event.

Coffee and tea

Ground coffee	125g (4oz) for 12 medium cups
Instant	75g (3oz) for 12 large cups
Milk	allow 450ml (¾ pint) for 12 cups of tea

Approximate Coffee and Tea Quantities

COFFEE GROUND

1 serving	200ml (7fl oz)
24–26 servings	250–275g (9–10oz) coffee
If you make the coffee in advance, strain it after infusion.	3.4 litres (6 pints) water
Reheat without boiling.	1.7 litres (3 pints) milk
	450g (1lb) sugar

Tea

INDIAN

1 serving	200ml (7fl oz)
24–26 servings	50g (2oz) tea
It is better to make tea in several pots rather	4.5 litres (8 pints) water
than in one outsized one.	900ml (1½ pints) milk
	450g (1lb) sugar

CHINA

1 serving	200ml (7fl oz)
24–26 servings	50g (2oz) tea
Infuse China tea for 2–3 minutes only.	5.1 litres (9 pints) water
Put a thin lemon slice in each cup before pouring.	2–3 lemons
Serve sugar separately.	450g (1lb) sugar

Irish or Gaelic Coffee

To serve one, you will need:

25ml (1fl oz) Irish whiskey
1 tsp brown sugar
85–125ml (3–4fl oz) hot double-strength black coffee
1–2 tbsp double cream, chilled

1 Gently warm a glass, pour in the whiskey and add the sugar.
2 Pour in black coffee to within 2.5cm (1in) of the brim and stir to dissolve the sugar.
3 Fill to the brim with the chilled cream, poured over the back of a spoon, and leave to stand for a few minutes.

Liqueur Coffee Around the World

The following are made as for Irish Coffee. Allow 25ml (1fl oz) of the liqueur or spirit to 125ml (4fl oz) of double-strength black coffee, with sugar to taste – usually about 1 tsp – and some thick double cream to pour on top; these quantities will make 1 glassful:

❑ Cointreau Coffee
   (made with Cointreau)
❑ Caribbean Coffee
   (made with rum)
❑ German Coffee
   (made with Kirsch)
❑ Normandy Coffee
   (made with Calvados)
❑ Russian Coffee
   (made with vodka)
❑ Calypso Coffee
   (made with Tia Maria)
❑ Witch's Coffee
   (made with strega; sprinkle a little grated lemon zest on top)
❑ Curaçao Coffee
   (made with curaçao; stir with a stick of cinnamon)

Garden Party

All these recipes are designed to take the stress out of cooking. Follow this triple-tested time plan using our get-ahead instructions – there'll be no last-minute dashing around when all your guests arrive, and you can be confident that all the food will be a success!

Up to two days ahead
- Make the Salmon Sandwich Stacks
- Make Triumphant Strawberry and Cream Jelly

Up to a day ahead
- Make the Coronation Chicken (but don't add the coriander)
- Make the Layered Omelette Cake
- Make the Cheese and Pickle Crown Bread
- Prepare The Perfect Victoria Sponge
- Prepare Individual Queen of Trifles

On the day
6 hours before your serve
- Prepare Individual Sausage and Egg Pies and cook now – or closer to serving time if you want to eat them warm

4 hours before you serve
- Make the Marmite Cheese Straws

2 hours before you serve
- Prepare the Light and Fresh Potato Salad
- Slice and then chill the Salmon Sandwich Stacks

30 minutes before you serve
- Complete Coronation Chicken
- Add the cress to the Light and Fresh Potato Salad
- Finish off The Perfect Victoria Sponge and Individual Queen of Trifles

When your guests arrive

- Hand round the nibbles
- Serve the main courses when you're ready!
- Remember to turn out the jelly before you serve the puddings.

Salmon Sandwich Stacks

🍴 **Hands-on time:** 10 minutes, plus chilling

500g (1lb 2oz) mascarpone

1 tbsp roughly chopped capers

finely grated zest and juice of 1 lemon

2 tbsp freshly chopped dill

1 tbsp milk

12 medium-cut slices white bread

350g (12oz) smoked salmon slices

1 Put the mascarpone, capers, lemon zest and juice, dill and milk into a large bowl and mix well. Lay the bread on a board and divide half the mascarpone mixture among the slices. Spread evenly to the edges of the bread.

2 Next, divide half the smoked salmon slices over the mascarpone, making sure the fish is in an even layer (use scissors to trim). Lay another piece of bread on top of each stack and repeat the process with the remaining mascarpone mixture, smoked salmon and bread. Wrap the stacks individually in clingfilm and chill for at least 5 hours or ideally overnight.

3 Using a large serrated knife, cut the crusts off the sandwich stacks, then slice each stack into six rectangles. Secure each stack with a cocktail stick, if you like, and serve.

SAVE TIME

Stack, wrap and chill the sandwiches up to two days ahead. Slice the stacks into rectangles up to 2 hours ahead and keep chilled. Serve when ready.

Makes 24

Coronation Chicken

6 skinless chicken breasts

2 tsp mild curry powder

150g (5oz) mayonnaise

125g (4oz) crème fraîche

3 tbsp mango chutney

1 tsp Worcestershire sauce

2 celery sticks, finely chopped

75g (3oz) dried ready-to-eat apricots, chopped

50g (2oz) sultanas

50g (2oz) flaked almonds

a large handful of fresh coriander, chopped

salt and freshly ground black pepper

1 Put the chicken breasts into a large pan and cover with cold water. Bring to the boil, then reduce the heat and simmer gently for 15 minutes or until the chicken is cooked through (slice a breast in half to check). Drain and leave until completely cool.

2 Meanwhile, heat a small frying pan and toast the curry powder, stirring, until it smells fragrant – about 30 seconds. Empty into a large bowl and stir in the next seven ingredients, along with plenty of seasoning.

3 Cut or rip the cooled chicken into bite-size pieces and add to the mayonnaise mixture, along with most of the flaked almonds and chopped coriander. Stir well and check the seasoning.

4 To serve, garnish with the remaining almonds and coriander.

SAVE TIME

Prepare the chicken to the end of step 3 up to one day ahead, but don't add the coriander or garnish. Cover with clingfilm and chill. To serve, stir the chopped coriander through and complete the recipe.

Serves 12

Marmite Cheese Straws

Hands-on time: 10 minutes
Cooking time: about 20 minutes

2 × 375g sheets ready-rolled puff pastry
plain flour to dust
1½ tbsp Marmite
1½ tbsp milk
75g (3oz) each finely grated Parmesan
and Gruyère

1 Preheat the oven to 200°C (180°C fan oven) mark 6. Line baking sheets with baking parchment.
2 Unroll one puff pastry sheet on to a lightly floured worksurface. Put the Marmite into a small bowl and gradually mix in the milk. Brush half the mixture over the pastry.
3 Put both cheeses into another small bowl and stir to combine, then sprinkle half the cheese mixture over the pastry. Unroll the second puff pastry sheet and place on top of the cheese. Lightly roll a rolling pin over the pastry to stick the sheets together, rolling the pastry a little thinner in the process. Brush the top with the remaining Marmite mixture,

then sprinkle the remaining cheese over the top (pressing the cheese down to help it stick). Cut the pastry lengthways into 12 equal long strips, then halve to make 24 shorter strips.
4 Transfer the strips to the prepared baking sheets and cook for 15–20 minutes until golden brown. Transfer to a wire rack. Serve warm or at room temperature.

SAVE TIME

Make the cheese straws up to 4 hours ahead.

Makes 24

Individual Sausage and Egg Pies

Hands-on time: 30 minutes
Cooking time: about 40 minutes

7 small eggs

450g (1lb) sausage meat

1 tbsp wholegrain mustard

2 spring onions, finely chopped

1 tsp dried mixed herbs

plain flour to dust

about 1kg (2¼lb) shortcrust pastry

salt and freshly ground black pepper

1 Bring a large pan of water to the boil and add six of the eggs. Reduce the heat and simmer for exactly 6 minutes. Lift out of the pan with a slotted spoon and run them under cold water to cool quickly. Put to one side.

2 Put the sausage meat, mustard, spring onions, mixed herbs and some seasoning into a large bowl and mix well. Put to one side.

3 Preheat the oven to 220°C (200°C fan oven) mark 7. Lightly dust a worksurface with flour and roll out two-thirds of the pastry to 3mm (⅛in) thick. Stamp out twelve 10cm (4in) circles and press the circles into 12 holes of a deep muffin tin, working the pastry so that it comes just above the edges of the holes. Put the trimmings to one side.

4 Shell the eggs and halve lengthways through the yolk (which should not yet be completely set). Put one egg half, cut side down, in the bottom of each pastry well. Divide the sausage mixture among the wells, carefully pushing it around the eggs and levelling the surface.

5 Roll out the remaining one-third of the pastry and trimmings as before and stamp out 7.5cm (3in) circles. Beat the remaining egg and use some to brush the edges of the pies and the visible sausage meat. Press on the lids and seal the edges. Use a skewer to pierce a hole in the centre of each lid to let steam escape. If you like, re-roll any trimmings and use to decorate the pies. Brush the top of the pies with egg.

Serves 12

6 Cook the pies for 30–35 minutes until deep golden brown. Cool for 5 minutes in the tin, then remove from the tin and transfer the pies to a baking tray.

7 Cook the pies for a further 5 minutes to crisp up the edges. Cool for 10 minutes, then serve warm or at room temperature.

Layered Omelette Cake

16 large eggs

5 tbsp freshly chopped chives

2 tbsp vegetable oil

500g (1lb 2oz) full-fat cream cheese

1 red pepper, seeded and finely diced

½ red chilli, seeded and finely chopped (see Safety Tip, page 38)

50g (2oz) watercress, chopped, plus extra to garnish

salt and freshly ground black pepper

1 Beat the eggs in a large jug with 2 tbsp of the chives and plenty of seasoning. Heat ½ tbsp of the oil in a 20.5cm (8in) non-stick frying pan and pour in a quarter of the egg mixture. Swirl the pan to ensure the base is covered. Using a spatula, occasionally push the mixture in from the sides of the pan while it's cooking (but ensuring the base is always fully covered with egg). Cook for 2–3 minutes until the underneath is golden, then flip the omelette and cook for a further 2–3 minutes. Transfer the omelette to a plate to cool completely.

2 Repeat with the remaining oil and egg mixture to make three more omelettes (you may need to whisk the eggs before making each omelette to redistribute the chives).

3 While the omelettes are cooling, beat together the cream cheese, remaining chives, the red pepper, chilli, chopped watercress and some seasoning in a large bowl. Line a 20.5cm (8in) cake tin with clingfilm and place a cooled omelette in the base. Spread a third of the cream cheese mixture over the omelette. Repeat the stacking and

SAVE TIME

Prepare the omelette cake to the end of step 3 up to one day ahead. Chill. Complete the recipe to serve.

Serves 12

spreading twice more and then top with the remaining omelette. Cover the tin with clingfilm and chill in the fridge for at least 30 minutes.

4 To serve, lift the omelette cake from the tin and peel off the clingfilm. Transfer to a serving plate or cake stand, garnish with watercress and serve in wedges.

Light and Fresh Potato Salad

1.5kg (3lb 2oz) new potatoes, unpeeled, chopped into bite-size pieces

100ml (3½fl oz) olive oil

2 tbsp wholegrain mustard

juice of ½ lemon

200g (7oz) radishes, thinly sliced

4 spring onions, thinly sliced

a punnet of cress

salt and freshly ground black pepper

1 Cook the potatoes in salted boiling water for 15–20 minutes until just tender but not breaking apart.

2 While the potatoes are cooking, whisk together the oil, mustard, lemon juice and plenty of seasoning.

3 Drain the potatoes and leave to steam-dry for 5 minutes, then put them back into the pan. Pour the dressing over and add the radishes and spring onions. Fold together, trying not to break up the potatoes.

4 Tip into a serving dish and scatter the leaves from a punnet of cress over the top.

SAVE EFFORT

Prepare the potato salad up to a couple of hours ahead, but do not add the cress. Transfer to a serving dish, cover with clingfilm and chill. Complete the recipe to serve.

Serves 12

Cheese and Pickle Crown Bread

Hands-on time: 30 minutes, plus rising
Cooking time: about 30 minutes, plus cooling

25g (1oz) butter

300ml (½ pint) milk

2 medium eggs

450g (1lb) strong plain flour, plus extra
to dust

1 tsp caster sugar

7g sachet fast-action yeast

1 tsp salt

150g (5oz) Branston pickle

150g (5oz) extra mature Cheddar, grated

oil to grease

SAVE TIME

Make up to a day ahead. Cool
completely, then wrap in foil. Unwrap
and serve.

1 Heat the butter in a small pan until
melted, then stir in the milk and heat
gently for 1 minute until just warm.
Beat in one of the eggs.

2 Put the flour, sugar, yeast and salt
into a bowl and stir together. Add
the milk mixture and stir quickly to
make a soft, but not sticky, dough (add
a little more milk/flour as needed).
Tip the dough on to a lightly floured
worksurface and knead for 10 minutes.
Form into a ball, cover with a clean
teatowel and leave to rise for 30
minutes.

3 Roll the dough out to make a 25.5 ×
38cm (10 × 15in) rectangle. Put the
pickle and cheese into a small bowl
and stir to mix, then spread the
mixture over the dough, leaving a
1cm (½in) border. Roll the dough up
from one of the long edges to make a
sausage shape. Use a bread knife to
cut into 12 slices. Flour a baking sheet,
then arrange the slices on their sides
(with the swirls facing sideways) and

just touching to make a ring shape on the baking sheet. Loosely cover with oiled clingfilm and leave to rise for 30 minutes.

4 Preheat the oven to 200°C (180°C fan oven) mark 6. Beat the remaining egg and use to glaze the rolls. Bake for 25–30 minutes until risen, golden and the rolls feel firm. Carefully transfer the ring to a wire rack and cool completely before serving.

The Perfect Victoria Sponge

Hands-on time: 30 minutes
Cooking time: about 30 minutes, plus cooling

225g (8oz) unsalted butter, softened, plus extra to grease

225g (8oz) self-raising flour, plus extra to dust

225g (8oz) caster sugar

4 medium eggs

1 tbsp milk

6 tbsp loose strawberry jam

250ml (8fl oz) double cream

icing sugar to dust

1 Preheat the oven to 180°C (160°C fan oven) mark 4. Lightly grease two 20.5cm (8in) sandwich tins and line the bases with baking parchment. Dust the sides of each tin with flour and tap out the excess.

2 Put the butter and caster sugar into a large bowl and beat together using a hand-held electric whisk until pale and fluffy – about 3 minutes. Gradually add the eggs, beating well after each addition (if the mixture looks as if it might curdle, mix in a few tablespoons of the flour).

3 Sift in the flour and fold together using a large metal spoon. Next, fold in the milk.

4 Divide the mixture equally between the prepared tins and level the surface of each. Bake in the centre of the oven for 25–30 minutes until the cakes are golden and springy to the touch when lightly pressed in the centre. Leave the cakes to cool in the tins for 5 minutes, then turn out, transfer to a wire rack and leave to cool completely.

5 Peel off the lining papers. Spread the jam over the top of one of the sponge cakes. Next, lightly whip the cream in a medium bowl and dollop over the jam layer. Top with the remaining sponge cake and dust with icing sugar. Serve in slices.

Cuts into 10 slices

Individual Queen of Trifles

Hands-on time: 30 minutes, plus chilling
Cooking time: about 10 minutes, plus cooling

300g (11oz) Madeira sponge cake

25–40ml (1–1½fl oz) cream sherry,
to taste, or orange juice

5 tbsp raspberry jam

300g (11oz) raspberries

4 tbsp custard powder

4 tbsp caster sugar

600ml (1 pint) milk

2 tsp vanilla extract

300ml (½ pint) double cream

2 tbsp icing sugar, sifted

about 50g (2oz) meringue nests,
crumbled

25g (1oz) shelled unsalted pistachios,
chopped

1 Slice the Madeira cake into 10 equal
slices and roughly crumble each slice
into the bottom of a tumbler or small
wine glass. Press down lightly. Divide
the sherry or orange juice among the
glasses, pouring it over the cake.

2 Heat the jam gently in a medium pan
until it loosens. Add the fresh raspberries
and gently stir to coat the berries in the
jam. Divide among the glasses.

3 Next, make the custard. Put the
custard powder and caster sugar into
a pan and gradually whisk in the
milk until smooth. Put the pan over
a medium heat and bring to the boil,
stirring constantly to prevent lumps,
then cook until the custard thickens.
Take off the heat and stir in the
vanilla. Leave to cool for 15 minutes.

4 Re-whisk the custard to break it up
and divide among the glasses. Chill
until needed.

5 To serve, lightly whip the cream and
icing sugar until the cream just holds
its shape. Divide among the glasses,
then scatter the meringues and
pistachios on top. Serve.

SAVE TIME

Prepare the trifles to the end of step
4 up to one day ahead. Complete
the recipe up to 1 hour ahead.

Serves 10

Triumphant Strawberry and Cream Jelly

Hands-on time: 20 minutes, plus chilling
Cooking time: about 5 minutes, plus cooling

2 × 135g packs strawberry jelly

1 tsp edible gold glitter (optional)

oil to grease (optional)

100g (3½oz) caster sugar

1 vanilla pod, split lengthways

300ml (½ pint) double cream

600ml (1 pint) milk

8 gelatine sheets

1. Snip the jelly into cubes and put into a large jug. Pour in 300ml (½ pint) boiling water and leave to dissolve, stirring occasionally. Top up the mixture with cold water to make 1.2 litres (2 pints). Stir in the glitter, if you like.

2. Pour the strawberry jelly mixture into a 2.7 litre (4¾ pint) non-stick kugelhopf mould or large bowl (if your bowl or mould is not non-stick, grease lightly with a mild oil). Chill until completely set – about 3 hours.

3. Meanwhile, put the sugar, vanilla pod, cream and milk into a pan and heat gently, whisking occasionally to help release the vanilla seeds, until the mixture just begins to boil. Take off the heat and leave to infuse for 15 minutes.

4. Put the gelatine sheets into a bowl, cover with cold water and leave to soak for 5 minutes. Lift the soaked gelatine out of the water (discard the water) and add to the cream pan, then stir to dissolve (if the cream mixture is not hot enough to dissolve the gelatine, then reheat gently until it dissolves).

5. Lift out the vanilla pod and leave the cream mixture until completely cool – the strawberry jelly needs to be fully set before proceeding.

SAVE TIME

Make the jelly to the end of step 5 up to two days ahead. Chill. Complete the recipe to serve.

118

Serves 10

6 Gently pour the cream mixture over the set jelly and leave in the fridge to set completely – about 5 hours.

7 To serve, turn the jelly out on to a serving plate. If it doesn't come out easily, dip the base of the mould briefly into a bowl of hot water (taking care no water comes in contact with the jelly). Turn out the jelly and serve.

Buffet Food

Perfect Buffet Party

Use this handy guide to help you work out quantities of starters, main dishes, vegetables and dressings for your buffet party.

Starters	Portions	Ingredients	Notes
FISH COCKTAIL	1	50g (2oz) peeled shrimps, prawns, crab or lobster meat, 2 lettuce leaves, about 40ml (1½fl oz) sauce	Serve in stemmed glasses, garnished with a shrimp or prawn. Serve with lemon wedges.
	12	700g (1½lb) fish (as above), 1 large lettuce, 450ml (¾ pint) sauce	
PÂTÉS allow 3 half slices hot toast per person to serve with the pâté	1	75-125g (3-4oz)	
	12	1.1kg (2½lb)	
SMOKED SALMON (serve with toast as above or brown bread)	1	40-50g (1½-2oz)	
	12	550g (1¼lb)	
	25	1.1kg (2½lb)	
OTHER SMOKED FISH such as smoked trout or mackerel	1	125g (4oz)	
	12	1.1kg (2½lb)	
	25	2-2.5kg (4½-5½lb)	
SOUPS cream, clear or iced	1	150-200ml (5-7fl oz)	
	12	2.3 litres (4 pints)	
	25	4.5 litres (8 pints)	

	Portions	Ingredients	Notes
Main dishes			
DELICATESSEN MEATS ham, tongue, salami	1 12 25	75-125g (3-4oz) 1kg (2¼lb) 2.3kg (5lb)	
SALMON	1 12	125-175g (4-6oz) 1.4-1.8kg (3-4lb)	
ROAST TURKEY	10-15 20-30	3.6-5kg (8-11lb) 6.8-9kg (15-20lb)	
CHICKEN joint whole	1 24-26	150-225g (5-8oz) three 2.7kg (6lb) birds	Serve hot or cold.
Salad vegetables and dressings			
CARROTS	12 25	900g (2lb), grated 1.8kg (4lb), grated	
CELERY	12 25	2-3 heads 5 heads	
CUCUMBERS	12 25	1-1½ cucumbers 2-3 cucumbers	
LETTUCE	12 25	2-3 lettuces 5-6 lettuces	Dress at last minute.
BOILED POTATOES	12 25	700g (1½lb) 1.4kg (3lb)	For potato salads.
TOMATOES	12 25	700g (1½lb) 1.4kg (3lb)	
FRENCH DRESSING	12 25	300ml (½ pint) 450-600ml (¾-1 pint)	
MAYONNAISE	12 25	600ml (1 pint) 900ml-1 litre (1½-1¾pints)	

Perfect Buffet Party

Use this handy guide to help you work out quantities of desserts, savouries, bread, crackers, sandwiches, butter and cheese for your buffet party.

Desserts	Portions	Ingredients	Notes
MERINGUES	40 (small meringue halves)	6 egg whites, 350g (12oz) caster sugar, 600ml (pint) whipped cream	Sandwich meringue halves together with the whipped cream not more than 2 hours before serving.
PROFITEROLES	6	1 quantity of Choux pastry, 150ml (¼ pint) whipped cream, 1 quantity of Rich Chocolate Sauce	Fill the profiteroles with the whipped cream not more than 2 hours before serving.
	12–15	2 quantities of Choux pastry, 300ml (¼ pint) whipped cream, 2 quantities of Chocolate Sauce	
ICE CREAM (bought or homemade)	12 25–30	1 litre (1¾ pints) 2.3 litres (4 pints)	Transfer from the freezer to the fridge 30 minutes before serving.
Savouries			
CHEESE STRAWS	48	Cheese Straws x 2	
SAUSAGE ROLLS	64	Sausage Rolls x 4	

	Portions	Ingredients	Notes
RED PEPPER PESTO CROÛTES	48	Red Pepper Pesto Croûtes x 2	
COCKTAIL SAUSAGES	32	450g (1lb)	
QUICHE	6–8	20.5cm (8in) quiche	

Bread, Crackers and Sandwiches

	Portions	Ingredients	Notes
BREAD LOAVES	10–12 slices	1 small loaf, about 400g (14oz)	
	20–24 slices	1 large loaf, about 800g (1lb 12oz)	
	50 slices	1 long sandwich loaf, 1.4kg (3lb)	
SLICES OF BREAD	1	1–1½ slices	Cut into triangles when serving with a meal.
FRENCH BREAD	6–8	1 small loaf	
	12–15	1 large loaf	
CHEESE BISCUITS OR CRACKERS	1	3 biscuits	
	30	60 biscuits	

Butter

	Portions	Ingredients	Notes
	1	15–25g (½–1oz) butter	If bread is served with the meal.
	1	25–40g (1–1½oz) butter	If serving cheese as a course.
spreads 10–12 sandwiches		About 125g (4oz) butter	
spreads 10–12 bread rolls		About 125g (4oz) butter	

Cheese

	Portions	Ingredients	Notes
CHEESE (for biscuits)	1	25–40g (1–1½oz)	Serve a selection of at least four types.
	25	700–900g (1½–2lb)	
CHEESE (for wine and cheese parties)	1	75g (3oz)	
	25	2–2.3kg (4½–5lb)	

Fresh and Fruity Barley Salad

Hands-on time: 15 minutes
Cooking time: about 25 minutes

250g (9oz) pearl barley
125g (4oz) tenderstem broccoli, trimmed
2 peaches
½ cucumber, seeded and diced
a small handful of fresh mint, roughly chopped
50g (2oz) rocket
410g can chickpeas, drained and rinsed
2 tbsp balsamic vinegar
1 tbsp extra virgin olive oil
salt and freshly ground black pepper

1 Put the pearl barley into a large pan and cover well with water. Add some salt and bring to the boil, then reduce the heat and simmer for about 25 minutes or until the barley is just tender. Add the tenderstem broccoli for the final 3 minutes of cooking. Drain and sput to one side.

2 Meanwhile, peel and halve the peaches and discard the stones. Cut each peach half into four wedges, then put the wedges into a large serving bowl. Add the cucumber, mint, rocket and chickpeas.

3 Add the balsamic vinegar, oil and some seasoning to the peach bowl, then lightly mix through the drained barley mixture. Check the seasoning and serve.

Serves 4

Classic Coleslaw

Hands-on time: 15 minutes

¼ each medium red and white
  cabbage, shredded

1 carrot, grated

20g (¾oz) fresh flat-leafed parsley,
  finely chopped

For the dressing

1½ tbsp red wine vinegar

4 tbsp olive oil

½ tsp Dijon mustard

salt and freshly ground black pepper

1 To make the dressing, put the
  vinegar into a small bowl, add the
  oil, mustard and plenty of seasoning.
  Mix well.

2 Put the cabbage and carrot into a
  large bowl and toss to combine.
  Add the parsley.

3 Stir the dressing again, pour over
  the cabbage mixture and toss well to
  coat.

SAVE EFFORT

For an easy way to get a brand
new dish, make this into
Thai-style Coleslaw: replace the
red cabbage with a good handful
of fresh bean sprouts, the parsley
with freshly chopped coriander,
and add 1 seeded and finely
chopped red chilli (see Safety Tip,
page 38). For the dressing, replace
the vinegar with lime juice, the
olive oil with toasted sesame oil
and the mustard with soy sauce.

Serves 6

Jumbo Salmon Blini

Hands-on time: 20 minutes
Cooking time: about 10 minutes, plus cooling

300ml (½ pint) crème fraîche

grated zest and juice of ½ lemon, plus lemon wedges to serve (optional)

175g (6oz) plain flour

1 tsp baking powder

3 large eggs, separated

200ml (7fl oz) milk

3 tbsp chopped fresh chives, plus extra to garnish

½ tbsp olive oil

210g pack smoked salmon slices

salt and freshly ground black pepper

1 tbsp lumpfish caviar to garnish (optional)

1 Mix the crème fraîche, lemon zest and juice, and seasoning together in a small bowl. Put to one side.

2 Sift the flour, baking powder and a pinch of salt into a large bowl. Make a well in the centre and add the egg yolks and milk. Gradually whisk the flour into the liquid to make a smooth batter.

3 In a separate bowl, whisk the egg whites until they form stiff peaks. Use a large metal spoon to fold the egg whites into the batter, then add the chives and some pepper.

4 Preheat the grill to medium. Heat the oil in a 25.5cm (10in) non-stick frying pan. Add the batter and cook over a low-medium heat for 3–4 minutes until the base is golden. Next, grill for 3 minutes until golden and cooked through. Leave the blini to cool for 30 minutes.

5 To serve, put the blini on to a cake stand or serving plate and spoon over the crème fraîche mixture. Top with smoked salmon and garnish with extra chives, pepper and lumpfish caviar, if you like. Serve with lemon wedges, if you like.

Serves 8

Broccoli, Gorgonzola and Walnut Quiche

Hands-on time: 15 minutes, plus chilling
Cooking time: about 1 hour

400g (14oz) shortcrust pastry

plain flour to dust

150g (5oz) broccoli florets

100g (3½oz) Gorgonzola, crumbled

2 medium eggs, plus 1 medium
   egg yolk

300ml (½ pint) double cream

25g (1oz) roughly chopped
   walnut halves

salt and freshly ground black pepper

1 Preheat the oven to 200°C (180°C fan oven) mark 6. Roll out the pastry on a lightly floured worksurface until the thickness of a £1 coin, then use to line a 23cm (9in) × 2.5cm (1in) deep fluted tart tin. Prick the base all over and chill for 15 minutes. Bake blind for 20 minutes then remove the paper and beans and bake for 5 minutes. Lower the oven setting to 150°C (130°C fan oven) mark 2.

2 Cook the broccoli in boiling water for 3 minutes, then drain and dry on kitchen paper. Arrange the broccoli in the pastry case and dot with the Gorgonzola. Whisk together the eggs and egg yolk, cream and seasoning, then pour into the case. Scatter the chopped walnut halves over the surface.

3 Cook the quiche for 40 minutes or until the filling is set. Serve warm or at room temperature.

FREEZE AHEAD

To freeze, complete the recipe up to one month in advance. Cool the quiche in the tin, then wrap in clingfilm and freeze.

To use, thaw completely, then serve at room temperature, or gently reheat for 20 minutes in an oven preheated to 150°C (130°C fan oven) mark 2.

Serves 6

Bean and Broccoli Filo Tart

🍴 **Hand-on time:** 20 minutes
Cooking time: about 40 minutes

2 medium eggs
250g (9oz) crème fraîche
150g (5oz) soya beans, frozen
100g (3½oz) broccoli, cut into
  small florets
75g (3oz) sunblush tomatoes, chopped
75g (3oz) feta, crumbled
small handful of fresh mint
  leaves, chopped
6 sheets filo pastry (270g pack)
sunflower oil to brush
salt and freshly ground black pepper
green salad to serve

Make tart up to a day ahead. Cool
in the tin, cover with foil and chill.
Serve cold or reheat (covered) for
15–20 minutes in oven preheated to
180°C (160°C fan oven) mark 4.

1 Preheat the oven to 180°C (160°C fan oven) mark 4. In a large bowl, beat together the eggs, crème fraîche and some seasoning. In a separate bowl, mix together the soya beans, broccoli, tomatoes, feta and mint. Add three-quarters of the mixture to the egg.

2 Brush the top of one of the filo sheets with oil, then lay it in a 20.5cm (8in) round loose-bottomed cake tin, letting the excess hang over the sides. Repeat with remaining sheets, overlapping the sheets slightly each time (there should be no gaps). Pour in the crème fraîche mixture, then scatter over the remaining vegetable mix.

3 Crumple the overhanging pastry down inside the tin (above the level of the filling) and brush the pastry with oil. Put the tin on a baking sheet and cook for 35–40 minutes or until filling is set and the pastry is golden. Serve warm or at room temperature with a green salad.

Perfect Cheese

Probably the best place to buy cheese is from a specialist cheese shop if you are lucky enough to have access to one, otherwise many supermarkets have a fresh cheese counter offering a good variety of farmhouse and factory-made cheeses.

Buying and storing cheese

Try to taste first before you commit to buying a cheese, as artisan cheeses will vary within, as well as across, varieties – some cheeses differ according to the time of year, and certain varieties are seasonal. Once you have made your choice, make sure the cheese is freshly sliced to your requirements. Buy only as much or as little as you think you need – central heating and refrigeration will dry out the cheese once you get it home.

The best way to store cheese is to wrap it in waxed paper then to put into an unsealed plastic food bag or cheese box. Keep in the fridge in the least cold area away from the freezer compartment. If you have a whole, rinded cheese, cover the cut surface with clingfilm.

To enjoy cheese at its best, you should always remove it from the fridge at least 2 hours before serving to bring it to room temperature. Loosen the wrapping and remove it just before serving. Provide at least two knives for cutting, so that there is a separate one for blue cheese.

Buying cheese for vegetarians

Some vegetarians prefer to avoid cheeses that have been produced by the traditional method, because this uses animal-derived rennet; however, most supermarkets and cheese shops now stock an excellent range of vegetarian cheeses, produced using vegetarian rennet. Always check the label when buying.

Selecting for a cheeseboard

Choosing cheeses for a cheeseboard is a matter of satisfying everyone's taste, so a range of flavours from mild to strong, and a variety of textures, is important. Think about shapes and colours, too. If you are serving four cheeses, choose one hard, one soft, one blue and one goat's cheese.

If you are buying from a specialist cheese shop or a supermarket cheese counter, ask to try a piece first so that you know what you are getting and can balance the flavours. It is a question of quality rather than quantity, as a few excellent cheeses are more appealing than five or six with competing flavours.

To accompany your cheeses, choose crisp apples, juicy pears, grapes or figs. Very mild, soft goat's cheeses can be eaten with strawberries; slightly harder ones go well with cherry tomatoes or olives. Salad leaves should be bitter – try some chicory, frisée or rocket. Walnuts and celery are excellent with blue cheese. Oatcakes, wheat wafers and digestive biscuits go well with most cheeses, and if you want to serve bread, make sure it is fresh and crusty. Butter should be unsalted.

As for when you serve cheese, rounding off the meal with the cheeseboard is the norm in this country, but the French custom of moving from main course to cheese course is worth considering. It enables you to savour the cheeses before you are too full to enjoy them, and you can carry on eating with the same wine.

Chicken and Vegetable Terrine

Hands-on time: 40 minutes, plus chilling
Cooking time: 1 hour 2 minutes, plus cooling

900g (2lb) chicken joints
1 small slice of white bread,
   crusts removed
450ml (¾ pint) double cream, chilled
1 small bunch of watercress
125g (4oz) small young carrots
125g (4oz) French beans, trimmed
   and stringed
275g (10oz) peas in the pod, shelled
75g (3oz) small even-sized
   button mushrooms
200g (7oz) can artichoke hearts,
   drained
butter to grease
salt and freshly ground black pepper
rocket leaves to garnish (optional)

For the sauce

225g (8oz) ripe tomatoes, skinned
   and quartered
125ml (4fl oz) vegetable oil
50ml (2fl oz) white wine vinegar
75ml (2½fl oz) tomato purée

1 Cut all the chicken flesh away from the chicken bones; discard the skin and any fat. Finely mince the chicken and the bread. Chill for 30 minutes. Stir the cream, a little at a time, into the chicken mixture with salt and ground black pepper to taste.

2 Trim the watercress and discard the coarse stalks. Stir one-third of the chicken mixture into the watercress. Cover both bowls and chill for 2 hours.

3 Preheat the oven to 170°C (150°C fan oven) mark 3. The careful preparation of vegetables is essential to the final presentation. Cut the carrots into neat matchstick pieces, 2.5cm (1in) by 3mm (⅛in). Cut the beans into similar-length pieces. Blanch the carrots, beans and peas for 2 minutes in separate pans of boiling water. Drain.

4 Trim the mushroom stalks level with the caps. Cut the mushrooms across

into slices 5mm (¼in) thick. Dice the artichoke hearts into 5mm (¼in) pieces.

5 Grease a 1.1 litre (2 pint) lidded terrine dish and base line with a rectangular piece of paper, grease the top of the paper. Take half the watercress and chicken mixture and spread it evenly over the base of the terrine. Arrange the carrots in neat crossways lines over the top, then spread one-quarter of the chicken mixture carefully over the carrots.

6 Lightly seasoning the vegetables as they are layered, sprinkle the peas over the chicken mixture in the dish and put another thin layer of chicken mixture on top. Next, put the mushrooms in crossways lines and top with the remaining watercress and chicken mixture. Arrange the artichokes on top, cover with half the remaining chicken mixture, arrange the beans in crossways lines, and cover with the remaining chicken mixture.

7 Put a double sheet of greased greaseproof paper on top and cover tightly with the lid. Put the terrine in a roasting tin with water to come halfway up the side. Cook in the oven for 1 hour or until firm.

8 Cool a little, drain off any juices, then invert the terrine on to a serving plate. Cool, then chill for 1 hour before serving.

9 Meanwhile, to make the sauce, purée the tomatoes in a blender or food processor with the oil, vinegar, tomato purée and seasoning. Rub through a sieve. Chill lightly before serving, then garnish the terrine with some rocket leaves, if you like.

Serves 8

139

Raised Pork Pie

Hands-on time: 45 minutes, plus chilling
Cooking time: about 3½ hours, plus cooling

3 or 4 small veal bones
1 small onion, peeled
1 bay leaf
4 black peppercorns
900g (2lb) boneless leg or shoulder
  of pork, cubed
¼ tsp cayenne pepper
¼ tsp ground ginger
¼ tsp ground mace
¼ tsp dried sage
¼ tsp dried marjoram
1 tbsp salt
½ tsp ground black pepper
300ml (½ pint) milk and water mixed
150g (5oz) lard
450g (1lb) plain flour, plus extra to dust
1 medium egg, beaten
salad to serve

1 Put the bones, onion, bay leaf and peppercorns in a pan and cover with water. Simmer for 20 minutes, then boil to reduce the liquid to 150ml (¼ pint). Strain and cool.

2 Mix the pork with the spices and herbs, 1 tsp salt and the pepper.

3 Bring the milk, water and lard to the boil in a pan, then gradually beat it into the flour and the remaining salt in a bowl. Knead for 3–4 minutes.

4 Roll out two-thirds of the pastry on a lightly floured surface and mould into a 20.5cm (8in) base-lined, springform cake tin. Cover and chill for 30 minutes. Keep the remaining pastry covered. Preheat the oven to 220°C (200°C fan oven) mark 7.

5 Spoon the meat mixture and 4 tbsp cold stock into the pastry case. Roll out the remaining pastry to make a lid and put on top of the meat mixture, sealing the pastry edges well. Decorate with pastry trimmings and make a hole in the centre.

Serves 8

Glaze with the beaten egg.

6 Bake for 30 minutes. Cover loosely
  with foil, lower the oven setting to
  180°C (160°C fan oven) mark 4 and
  bake for a further 2½ hours. Cool.

7 Warm the remaining jellied stock
  until liquid, then pour into the
  centre hole of the pie. Chill and
  serve with salad.

SAVE EFFORT

If you have no bones available for
stock, use 2 tsp gelatine to 300ml
(½ pint) stock.

Strawberry Pavlova with Rosewater Syrup

Hands-on time: 20 minutes
Cooking time: about 40 minutes, plus cooling

10 medium egg whites
600g (1lb 5oz) caster sugar
1¾ tbsp cornflour
1kg (2¼lb) strawberries, hulled
150ml (¼ pint) dessert wine, such as
   Muscat de Beaumes de Venise
1 tsp rose water
600ml (1 pint) double cream
3 tbsp icing sugar, sifted

1 Preheat the oven to 150°C (130°C fan oven) mark 2. Line a large baking sheet with baking parchment. Use a pencil to draw a 28cm (11in) diameter circle on the parchment, then flip it over so the pencil mark is underneath.

2 Using electric beaters, whisk the egg whites in a large, grease-free bowl until stiff but not dry. Gradually add 550g (1¼lb) caster sugar, whisking all the time, until the mixture is stiff and glossy. Quickly beat in 1 tbsp cornflour.

SAVE EFFORT

Cook the meringue, make the strawberry syrup and hull the strawberries up to one day ahead. Cool the meringue on the baking sheet, then cover with clingfilm and store at room temperature. Cool the syrup, then cover and chill. Keep the hulled strawberries covered in the fridge. Whip the cream mixture up to 2 hours ahead, then chill. To serve, bring the syrup, strawberries and cream up to room temperature, then complete the recipe.

3 Spoon the mixture on to the prepared baking tray within the marked circle, pushing it into peaks at the edges of the circle. Bake for 40 minutes or until the meringue is firm to the touch and peels away

Serves 10

from the parchment. Transfer to a rack and leave to cool.

4 Meanwhile, put 200g (7oz) strawberries with the wine, remaining caster sugar and the rose water into a pan. Heat and simmer gently for 5 minutes. Blend until smooth, then push through a fine sieve, discarding the pips. Return the mixture to the pan and whisk in the remaining cornflour. Heat gently for 3–4 minutes until the syrup thickens, whisking constantly to remove any lumps. Take off the heat and leave to cool.

5 Transfer the cooled meringue to a serving plate. Gently whip the cream with the icing sugar until it just holds its shape. Dollop on top of the meringue, then pile on the remaining strawberries. Drizzle the cooled syrup over and serve.

White Chocolate and Pistachio Profiteroles

Hands-on time: 30 minutes
Cooking time: about 30 minutes, plus cooling

60g (2½oz) butter, cubed, plus extra
  to grease

75g (3oz) plain flour

2 medium eggs, well beaten

50g (2oz) pistachios

75g (3oz) white chocolate, chopped

450ml (¾ pint) double cream

3 tbsp icing sugar

1 Put the butter and 125ml (4fl oz) water into a large pan. Gently heat to melt the butter, then bring to the boil. Take off the heat, then quickly whisk in the flour. Carry on whisking until the mixture comes away from the sides of the pan (about 30 seconds). Cool for 15 minutes.

2 Preheat the oven to 200°C (180°C fan oven) mark 6 and lightly grease two baking sheets. Gradually whisk the eggs into the pan containing the cooled flour mixture, beating after each addition. Dollop teaspoonfuls of mixture on the baking sheets, spacing them well apart (you should have about 24). Use a damp finger to smooth the tops, then bake for about 25 minutes or until puffed and a deep golden colour.

3 Take out of the oven and pierce a hole in the bottom of each profiterole with a metal skewer – this will allow steam to escape. Transfer to a wire rack and leave to cool completely.

4 Meanwhile, put the pistachios into a food processor and whiz until finely ground. Put to one side. Melt half the white chocolate in a heatproof bowl set over a pan of gently simmering water, making sure the base of the bowl doesn't touch the water. Leave to cool for about 10 minutes.

5 Put the cream and icing sugar into a large bowl and whip until the mixture holds soft peaks. Whisk in half the ground pistachios and the cooled melted chocolate. Insert a 5mm (¼in) nozzle into a piping bag,

Serves 8

then fill the bag with the cream and pipe into the cooled profiteroles via the steam hole.

6 Stack the profiteroles on a serving plate. Melt the remaining white chocolate as before, then drizzle over the profiteroles. Scatter the remaining pistachios over them and serve.

SAVE EFFORT

For convenience, complete the recipe to the end of step 5 up to one day in advance, then chill. Complete the recipe up to 3 hours ahead and chill until ready to serve.

Rose Chocolates

Hands-on time: 10 minutes, plus freezing
Cooking time: about 1 minute

50g (2oz) white chocolate, chopped
50g (2oz) milk chocolate, chopped
50g (2oz) plain chocolate, chopped
a selection of sprinkles, coloured
   sugar, gold leaf and sugar roses
   to decorate

1 Put each type of chocolate into a small, microwave-safe bowl. Put the bowls side by side in the microwave and heat on full power for 1 minute. Continue heating for 10 second bursts until the chocolates are melted and smooth (you may need to take them out at different times).

2 Meanwhile, line two baking sheets with baking parchment. Drop scant teaspoonfuls of the different types of melted chocolate on to the prepared sheets, spacing a little apart, then smooth into rounds with the back of a teaspoon.

3 Decorate the chocolates with sprinkles, coloured sugar, gold leaf and sugar roses. Put in the freezer for 10 minutes to set, then pack into a tissue-lined box and serve with coffee.

Makes about 36

Drink Me

Wine and Drinks Guide

Use this handy guide to help you work out how much alcohol to factor in for your event.

- For large gatherings, offer one white and one red wine, sticking to around 12.5% alcohol, and have plenty of different soft drinks. Provide beer and lager if you like, but avoid spirits. Wines, sparkling wines, and hot or cold punches are ideal party drinks.

- For very large numbers, buy wines and champagne on a sale-or-return basis from a wine merchant. Mineral water, fruit juices and soft drinks can also be bought in this way. Most supermarkets will also allow this, provided the returned bottles are undamaged – check first.

- Wine boxes are good value and it is worth asking your local wine merchant for their advice – some are better than others. If you prefer to serve wine from the bottle, look at the cost-saving potential of buying by the case.

- When it comes to choosing wine it makes sense to find a supplier you can trust, whether it be a supermarket, wine merchant or warehouse. If you opt for something different, just buy one bottle and see if you enjoy it.

- Generally, red wine goes best with red meats, and white wine is the better complement to fish, chicken and light meats, but there really are no longer any hard-and-fast rules.

- For an aperitif, it is nice to serve a glass of chilled champagne or sparkling wine, or a dry sherry.

- Avoid sweet drinks, or spirits with a high alcohol content, as these tend to take the edge off the appetite, rather than stimulating it. Wine or sherry can be served with a soup course. A full-bodied red wine is an excellent accompaniment to the cheeseboard, although some people prefer to drink port with their cheese. You may wish to serve a dessert wine, such as

Sauternes, or a glass of fruity demi-sec champagne Coffee follows, with brandy and liqueurs if you like.

How much to buy?

If you allow one 75cl bottle of wine per head you should have more than enough. One standard 75cl bottle of wine, champagne or sparkling wine will give six glasses. A litre bottle will provide eight glasses. For a dinner party, allow one or two glasses of wine as an aperitif, one or two glasses with the first course, two glasses with the main course and another with the dessert or cheese.

Remember to buy plenty of mineral water – sparkling and still – and fresh fruit juices. For every ten guests, buy two 1.5 litre bottles of sparkling water and three similar-sized bottles of still water.

Serving wine

Warm white wine and champagne is inexcusable, and chilled red wine (unless young and intended for serving cold) is not at all pleasant. The ideal temperature for red wine is around 15–18°C, with the more tannic wines benefiting from the higher temperature. On a warm day, a brief spell in the fridge will help red wine. For whites, the more powerful wines, like Chardonnay, should be served cool rather than cold, at around 11–15°C, while other whites should be properly cold, at around 6–10°C. Party food will probably take up your available fridge space, so you will need plenty of ice to keep drinks cool.

If you have a lot of wine to chill, use the bath, or a large deep sink if you have one. About an hour before the party, half-fill the bath with ice, pour in some cold water and stand the bottles upright, making sure the ice and water come up to their necks. Alternatively, use a clean plastic dustbin or cool boxes as containers. (Some hire companies will loan special plastic bins for cooling wines.)

A large block of ice added to chilled water is a good idea. Make this by filling a large strong plastic bag with water, seal securely and place in the freezer until frozen.

Elderflower Fizz

🍴 **Hands-on time:** 1 minute

about 200ml (7fl oz) cloudy apple juice
100ml (4fl oz) elderflower liqueur
chilled sparkling white or rosé wine
apple slices and mint sprigs to garnish

1 Half-fill four champagne flutes with
   the cloudy apple juice, then add a
   quarter of elderflower liqueur to
   each glass and top up with chilled
   sparkling wine.
2 Garnish with a slice of apple and a
   sprig of mint.

HEALTHY TIP

For a thirst-quenching non-
alcoholic elderflower fizz, just
replace the wine with chilled
sparkling water.

Serves 4

Champagne Cocktail

TAKE
5

🍴 **Hands-on time:** 5 minutes

125ml (4fl oz) Grand Marnier
75ml (2½fl oz) grenadine
1 large orange, cut into 8 wedges
8 sugar cubes or sugar sticks
75cl bottle champagne, cava or other
  sparkling wine, chilled

1 Measure out the Grand Marnier and grenadine and divide among eight champagne glasses. Add an orange wedge and a sugar cube or stick to each glass.
2 Top up the glasses with the champagne, cava or sparkling wine and serve immediately.

Serves 8

Take 5 Classic Cocktails

Whisky Sour

To serve one you will need:
juice of ½ lemon, 1 tsp sugar, 25ml
(1fl oz) rye whisky and crushed ice.

1 Mix together the lemon juice,
   sugar and whisky, and shake
   well with the ice.
2 Serve in a whisky tumbler.

Margarita

To serve one you will need:
25ml (1fl oz) lemon or lime juice,
plus extra for dipping, 125ml (4fl oz)
tequila and 25ml (1fl oz) curaçao,
salt.

1 Dip the edges of a chilled glass
   into lemon juice and then salt.
2 In a shaker, mix the tequila,
   curaçao and lemon or lime juice.
3 Strain into the chilled glass and
   serve immediately.

Buck's Fizz

To serve one you will need:
juice from 1 small orange and 150ml
(¼ pint) champagne.

1 Strain the orange juice into a
   champagne flute and top up with
   chilled champagne. Serve at
   once.

Piña Colada

To serve one you will need:
85ml (3fl oz) white rum, 125ml
(4fl oz) pineapple juice, 50ml (2fl
oz) coconut cream, crushed ice,
1 pineapple slice and 1 cherry to
decorate.

1 Blend together the rum,
   pineapple juice, coconut cream
   and the crushed ice.
2 Pour into a large goblet or a
   hollowed-out pineapple half.
3 Decorate with a slice of
   pineapple and a cherry. Serve
   with straws.

Daiquiri

To serve one you will need:
juice of ½ lime or ¼ lemon, 1 tsp
sugar, 25ml (1fl oz) white rum,
crushed ice, extra fruit juice and
caster sugar to frost.

1 Mix the fruit juice, sugar and
   rum and shake well with the
   crushed ice in a shaker.
2 Dip the edges of the glass into
   a little more fruit juice and then
   into caster sugar to frost the rim
   before filling.

Alcoholic drinks and vegetarians

Animal-derived ingredients,
such as gelatine (from cattle) and
isinglass (from fish) are often used
as fining agents in wine, sherry,
port, beer and cider. For this reason
some vegetarians prefer to drink
only vegetarian alternatives. You
can find these in supermarkets and
online. Spirits (apart from some
malt whiskies, which have been
matured in sherry casks) and many
liqueurs are generally acceptable to
vegetarians.

Rum Punch

Hands-on time: 2 minutes

juice of 1 lime

2 tsp golden caster sugar

2 measures (50ml) dark rum

1 dash Angostura bitters

4–5 ice cubes

soda or mineral water, chilled

lime slices

1 Mix the lime juice and sugar in a tall glass. Add the rum, Angostura bitters and ice cubes.

2 Top up with soda or mineral water, add some slices of lime and serve immediately.

Serves 4

Cranberry Crush

Hands-on time: 5 minutes

75cl bottle sparkling wine, such as cava, chilled

300ml (½ pint) Calvados

1 litre (1¾ pints) cranberry juice, chilled

450ml (¾ pint) sparkling water, chilled

1 small orange, thinly sliced into rounds

10–12 ice cubes

1 Pour the sparkling wine, Calvados and cranberry juice into a large glass bowl.

2 Just before serving, pour in the sparkling water, stir, then add the orange slices and ice cubes. Ladle into glasses and serve immediately.

HEALTHY TIP

For an alternative flavour, use pomegranate juice instead of cranberry, and add a spoonful of fresh pomegranate seeds to each glass instead of orange slices.

Serves 14

Bloody Mary

Hands-on time: 2 minutes

1 tbsp Worcestershire sauce
1 dash Tabasco
1 measure (25ml) vodka, chilled
150ml (¼ pint) tomato juice, chilled
ice cubes
lemon juice to taste
celery salt to taste
1 celery stick, with the leaves left on, to serve

1 Pour the Worcestershire sauce, Tabasco, vodka and tomato juice into a tall glass and stir.
2 Add ice cubes and the lemon juice and celery salt to taste. Put the celery stick in the glass and serve.

HEALTHY TIP

For a Virgin Mary just omit the vodka to make this non-alcoholic cocktail.

Serves 1

Easy Eggnog

Hands-on time: 10 minutes

3 medium eggs
75g (3oz) caster sugar
50ml (2fl oz) brandy (optional)
100ml (3½fl oz) whole milk
freshly grated nutmeg, to garnish

1 Put the eggs into a large bowl.
Add the sugar and beat together
with an electric hand whisk until
thick and moussey, about 5 minutes.
With the motor running, quickly
add the brandy, if you like, followed
by the milk. Divide among eight
small glasses. Garnish with nutmeg
and serve.

Serves 8

Mulled Wine

Hands-on time: 10 minutes, plus infusing
Cooking time: about 15 minutes

2 oranges
6 cloves
75cl bottle fruity red wine
2 measures (50ml) brandy or Cointreau
1 cinnamon stick, broken
½ tsp mixed spice
2 tbsp golden granulated sugar

1 Cut one of the oranges into six wedges and push a clove into each wedge. Using a vegetable peeler, carefully pare the zest of the other orange into strips.

2 Put the clove-studded orange wedges in a stainless-steel pan, along with the red wine, brandy or Cointreau, cinnamon stick, mixed spice and sugar. Warm gently over a low heat for 10–15 minutes, then remove the pan from the heat and put to one side for 10 minutes to let the flavours infuse.

3 Strain the wine into a serving jug through a non-metallic sieve to remove the orange wedges and the cinnamon. Serve in heatproof glasses with a strip of orange zest draped over each glass.

SAVE TIME

Choose a bold, fruity red – nothing too oaky – such as Bordeaux or another wine made from Cabernet Sauvignon or Merlot.

Serves 6

Elderflower Cordial

To make about 1.1 litres (2 pints) you will need:
2kg (4½lb) golden granulated sugar, 80g (just over 3oz) citric acid , 2 medium lemons, sliced, 20 large young elderflower heads (shake to release any insects).

1   Bring 1.1 litres (2 pints) water to the boil, add the sugar and stir until dissolved.
2   Add the citric acid and lemon slices. Stir in the flower heads. Leave overnight, covered.
3   In the morning, sieve. If you want it clearer, strain again through muslin or a coffee filter. Bottle, give some away and keep the rest in the fridge – it will last for months!

Warming Ginger Soda

To serve six, you will need:
300g (11oz) unpeeled fresh root ginger, finely sliced, 225g (8oz) caster sugar, the grated zest and juice of 1½ lemons, 1 litre (1¾ pints) soda water.

1   Put the root ginger into a pan with the sugar and lemon zest and juice. Add about 600ml (1 pint) cold water to cover. Heat gently to dissolve the sugar, then turn up the heat and simmer for 10 minutes.
2   Strain through a fine sieve into a jug. Leave to cool for at least 10 minutes, then top up with soda water.

SAVE TIME

Make syrup up to three days ahead. Chill. Add soda to serve.

'Still' Lemonade

To make about 1.1 litres (2 pints),
you will need:
3 lemons, 175g (6oz) sugar.

1   Remove the lemon zest thinly
    with a potato peeler.
2   Put the zest and sugar into a
    bowl or large jug and pour on
    900ml (1½ pints) boiling water.
    Cover and leave to cool, stirring
    occasionally.
3   Add the juice of the lemons
    and strain the lemonade. Serve
    chilled.

Cranberry Cooler

To serve one you will need:
ice cubes, 75ml (2½fl oz) cranberry
juice, lemonade or sparkling water,
chilled, 1 lemon slice to serve.

1   Half-fill a tall glass with ice and
    pour in the cranberry juice.
2   Top up with lemonade. If you'd
    prefer the drink to be less sweet,
    double the amount of cranberry
    juice and top up with sparkling
    water. Stir well and serve with a
    slice of lemon.

Fruity Carrot with Ginger

To serve two you will need:
2 medium oranges, 1cm (½in)
piece fresh root ginger, peeled
and roughly chopped, 150ml (¼
pint) freshly pressed apple juice
or 2 dessert apples, juiced, 150ml
(¼ pint) freshly pressed carrot
juice or 3 medium carrots, 250g
(9oz), juiced, fresh mint leaves to
decorate.

1   Using a sharp knife, cut a
    slice of orange and put to one
    side for the decoration. Cut
    off the peel from the oranges,
    removing as much white pith as
    possible. Chop the flesh roughly,
    discarding any pips, and put
    into a blender. Add the chopped
    ginger.
2   Pour in the apple and carrot
    juice and blend until smooth.
    Divide between two glasses,
    decorate with quartered orange
    slices and a mint leaf and serve.

Calorie Gallery

398 cal ♥ 18g protein
15g fat (7g sat) ♥ 4g fibre
47g carb ♥ 2.5g salt

8

90 cal ♥ 2g protein
5g fat (1g sat) ♥ 0.5g fibre
10g carb ♥ 0.3g salt

10

90 cal ♥ 4g protein
6g fat (1g sat) ♥ 2g fibre
8g carb ♥ 0.3g salt

16

336 cal ♥ 11g protein
6g fat (1g sat) ♥ 2g fibre
62g carb ♥ 0.7 salt

18

147 cal ♥ 5g protein
13g fat (2g sat) ♥ 2g fibre
3g carb ♥ 0g salt

38

8 cal ♥ 0.1g protein
0g fat ♥ 0.2g fibre
2g carb ♥ 0.1g salt

40

43 cal ♥ 3g protein
2g fat (1g sat) ♥ 0.2g fibre
3g carb ♥ 0.2g salt

42

38 cal ♥ 2g protein
3g fat (1.5g sat) ♥ 0g fibre
0g carb ♥ 0.2g salt

52

42 cal ♥ 1g protein
3g fat (1g sat) ♥ 0.2g fibre
3g carb ♥ 0.2g salt

54

132 cal ♥ 3g protein
9g fat (3g sat) ♥ 0.4g fibre
11g carb ♥ 0.4g salt

56

302 cal ♥ 6g protein
17g fat (10g sat) ♥ 0.3g fibre
34g carb ♥ 0.2g salt

74

582 cal ♥ 9g protein
46g fat (23g sat) ♥ 1g fibre
35g carb ♥ 0.3g salt

76

for 10 slices: 363 cal
3g protein ♥ 18g fat (11g sat)
1g fibre ♥ 50g carb ♥ 0.4g salt

80

341 cal ♥ 4g protein
12g fat (7g sat) ♥ 0.8g fibre
58g carb ♥ 0.7g salt

82

195 cal ♥ 5g protein
1g fat (0.2g sat) ♥ 1g fibre
34g carb ♥ 0.3g salt

20

70 cal ♥ 3g protein
3g fat (1g sat) ♥ 1g fibre
9g carb ♥ 0.3g salt

24

72 cal ♥ 2g protein
2g fat (0.5g sat) ♥ 0.5g fibre
12g carb ♥ 0.3g salt

28

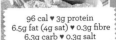

96 cal ♥ 3g protein
6.5g fat (4g sat) ♥ 0.3g fibre
6.3g carb ♥ 0.3g salt

30

140 cal ♥ 6g protein
10g fat (3g sat) ♥ 0.3g fibre
7g carb ♥ 0.6g salt

44

57 cal ♥ 2g protein
3g fat (2g sat) ♥ 0.3g fibre
6g carb ♥ 0.3g salt

46

52 cal ♥ 2g protein
3g fat (1g sat) ♥ 0.5g fibre
6g carb ♥ 0.1g salt

48

36 cal ♥ 1g protein
4g fat (0.5g sat) ♥ 0.1g fibre
1g carb ♥ 0.2g salt

50

105 cal ♥ 2g protein
7g fat (1g sat) ♥ 0.4g fibre
4g carb ♥ 0.3g salt

58

24 cal ♥ 3g protein
1g fat (0g sat) ♥ 0.1g fibre
0g carb ♥ 0.1g salt

60

without cream:
73 cal ♥ 2g protein
0g fat ♥ 0.8g fibre
18g carb ♥ 0g salt

62

without marzipan carrots:
697 cal ♥ 7g protein
48g fat (18g sat) ♥ 1g fibre
62g carb ♥ 0.9g salt

70

for 8 slices: 424 cal
5g protein ♥ 25g fat (13g sat)
5g fibre ♥ 46g carb ♥ 0.3g salt

84

185 cal ♥ 3g protein
1g fat (trace sat) ♥ 2g fibre
42g carb ♥ 0.1g salt

86

555 cal; 7g protein
31g fat (11g sat) ♥ 2g fibre
63g carb ♥ 0.5g salt

90

140 cal ♥ 3g protein
5g fat (3g sat) ♥ 0.9g fibre
22g carb ♥ 0.7g salt

92

140 cal ♥ 6g protein
11g fat (6g sat) ♥ 0.3g fibre
6g carb ♥ 0.8g salt

100

292 cal ♥ 21g protein
19g fat (5g sat) ♥ 0.8g fibre
10g carb ♥ 0.7g salt

102

150 cal ♥ 4g protein
10g fat (7g sat) ♥ 0.2g fibre
11g carb ♥ 0.5g salt

104

per pie: 508 cal ♥ 13g protein
35g fat (28g sat) ♥ 2g fibre
37g carb ♥ 2.0g salt

106

Calorie Gallery

229 cal ♥ 5g protein
6g fat (3g sat) ♥ 1g fibre
43g carb ♥ 0.4g salt

116

294 cal ♥ 5g protein
17g fat (11g sat) ♥ 0g fibre
31g carb ♥ 0.1g salt

118

371 cal ♥ 13g protein
7g fat (1g sat) ♥ 6g fibre
70g carb ♥ 0.5g salt

126

616 cal ♥ 19g protein
54g fat (23g sat) ♥ 4g fibre
8g carb ♥ 0.6g salt

138

617 cal ♥ 31g protein
37g fat (14g sat) ♥ 2g fibre
45g carb ♥ 2g salt

140

614 cal ♥ 5g protein
32g fat (20g sat) ♥ 1g fibre
78g carb ♥ trace salt

142

143 cal ♥ 0g protein
0g fat ♥ 0g fibre
8g carb ♥ 0g salt

158

114 cal ♥ 0g protein
0g fat ♥ 0g fibre
10g carb ♥ 0g salt

160

96 cal ♥ 0.3g protein
0g fat ♥ 0.2g fibre
9g carb ♥ 1.8g salt

162

90 cal ♥ 3g protein
3g fat (1g sat) ♥ 0g fibre
10g carb ♥ 0.1g salt

164

321 cal ♥ 12g protein
31g fat (15g sat) ♥ 0.3g fibre
1g carb ♥ 0.8g salt

149 cal ♥ 3g protein
7g fat (1g sat) ♥ 2g fibre
21g carb ♥ 0.3g salt

239 cal ♥ 10g protein
8g fat (4g sat) ♥ 1g fibre
34g carb ♥ 1.2g salt

527 cal ♥ 5g protein
35g fat (21g sat) ♥ 0.5g fibre
52g carb ♥ 0.3g salt

08

110

112

114

79 cal ♥ 0.5g protein
7g fat (1g sat) ♥ 1g fibre
3g carb ♥ 0.1g salt

306 cal ♥ 13g protein
20g fat (11g sat) ♥ 0.7g fibre
19g carb ♥ 1.6g salt

683 cal ♥ 12g protein
57g fat (27g sat) ♥ 2g fibre
33g carb ♥ 1g salt

298 cal ♥ 7g protein
21g fat (11g sat) ♥ 2g fibre
20g carb ♥ 0.7g salt

28

130

132

134

per profiterole:
496 cal ♥ 5g protein
44g fat (25g sat) ♥ 0.7g fibre
20g carb ♥ 0.3g salt

22 cal ♥ 0.3g protein
1.2g fat (0.7g sat) ♥ 0.1g fibre
3g carb ♥ 0g salt

112 cal ♥ 0.2g protein
0g fat ♥ 0g fibre
15g carb ♥ 0g salt

134 cal ♥ 0g protein
0g fat ♥ 0g fibre
16g carb ♥ 0g salt

44

146

152

154

120 cal ♥ 0g protein
0g fat ♥ 0g fibre
5g carb ♥ 0g salt

66

Index

PICTURE CREDITS
Photographers: Marie-Louise
Avery (pages 29 and 83); Nicki
Dowey (pages 9, 11, 15, 87, 129,
155, 159, 161, 163 and 167);
Will Heap (page 14); William
Lingwood (pages 75 and 78B);
Gareth Morgans (pages 17, 71, 81,
91, 127 and 153); Myles New (25,
26, 39, 41, 43, 47, 51, 53, 55, 57, 63,
101, 103, 105, 107, 109, 111, 113, 115,
117, 119, 133, 135 and 165); Craig
Robertson (pages 27, 32, 33, 78T
and 93); Sam Stowell (pages 45,
49, 59 and 61); Lucinda Symons
(pages 19, 21, 31, 77, 139 and 141);
Philip Webb (page 131);
Kate Whitaker (pages 85, 143,
145, and 147).

Home Economists:
Joanna Farrow, Emma Jane
Frost, Teresa Goldfinch, Alice
Hart, Lucy McKelvie, Kim
Morphew, Aya Nishimura,
Bridget Sargeson, Kate Trend
and Mari Mererid Williams.

Stylists: Tamzin Ferdinando,
Wei Tang, Helen Trent and
Fanny Ward.

BAKE ME A CAKE

There's always time for cake

EASY PEASY MEALS

Easy meals for every day

LET'S DO BRUNCH

Mouth-watering meals to start your day

CHEAP EATS

Budget-busting ideas that won't break the bank

SALAD DAYS

Oh-so-fresh ideas for fabulous salads

Available online at store.anovabooks.com and from all good bookshops

POSH NOSH

Delicious recipes to impress your guests

PARTY FOOD

Delicious recipes to get the party started

SLOW STOPPERS

Slow-cooked meals packed with flavour

GREAT VEG

Inspired ideas for delicious veggie meals

AL FRESCO EATS

Easy grills, barbecues and picnics

ROAST IT

There's nothing better than a delicious roast

FLASH IN THE PAN

Spice up your noodles and stir-fries

GLUTEN-FREE AND EASY

Oh-so-good-for-you recipes that taste great

LOW FAT LOW CAL

Nice recipes don't need to be naughty